There is no such th...
sovereignty of God t...
unanswered, or propose solutions that leave us wondering and
even protesting. Jamie Freeman's book is no exception. But it
is exceptional! And the reason is that, unlike so many books on
suffering, this author suffers. He doesn't write from an ivory
tower, insulated from the pain about which he speculates.
Jamie's battle with cerebral palsy is very real and life-long and
brings to his treatment of suffering a personal dimension so
lacking in most other books. To be able to say that his affliction
'was an act of the grace of God' tells you a lot about Jamie and
this book. You won't agree with everything he says, but he's
earned the right for you to hear him say it.

Sam Storms
Lead Pastor, Bridgeway Church
Oklahoma City, Oklahoma

Jamie Freeman's story is one of triumph over tragedy and
a wonderful testimony to God's power and grace in his life.
I highly recommend his book as he shares his story and probes
into the difficult and challenging discussion of theodicy or
the problem of suffering. Jamie's testimony and insights
will inspire and challenge you. His perseverance, optimistic
spirit, and genuine love for Jesus are an encouragement and
blessing to me.

Danny Forshee
Lead Pastor
Great Hills Baptist Church
Austin, Texas

Starting from his own suffering as a person born with cerebral palsy, Jamie Freeman has, by God's grace, thought, prayed, and wrestled his way through to a deeply biblical understanding of God's goodness in all of our suffering. Read this book and grow in grace. Meet Jamie and see that grace embodied in his walking and talking.

Mark R. Talbot
Associate Professor of Philosophy
Wheaton College
Wheaton, Illinois

The greatest contemporary challenge to authentic Christianity is not cultural disapproval, but popular distortion. The gospel that thrives in the face of persecution is lost by its dilution, particularly when presented as a means to achieve comfort and success instead of the forgiveness of sins and union with Christ. Many American churches now would rather attain the worldly wealth of Esau than abide in the weathered tents of Jacob as an heir of God's eternal promise. In *Though He Slay Me*, Jamie Freeman dares to stand on the platform of his own astonishing agony and prophetically summon each of us to exult in the sovereign reign of God wherever it leads, to find an opportunity for his glory in the most dire and difficult circumstances of life. His personal story is riveting, inspiring, challenging, and completely countercultural. This message will not be welcomed in some quarters, but it's right at home with the bloody cross of Jesus.

Hershael W. York
Victor & Louise Lester Professor of Preaching
The Southern Baptist Theological Serminary
Senior Pastor, Buck Run Baptist Church
Frankfort, Kentucky

Jamie Freeman

Though He Slay Me

Seeing God as Good in Suffering

CHRISTIAN
FOCUS

Jamie Freeman is a graduate of Oklahoma Baptist University. He seeks to proclaim the gospel of Christ and His Kingdom through writing and expositional preaching. Jamie lives in Arkansas with his wife and three sons.

Copyright © Jamie Freeman 2014

paperback ISBN 978-1-78191-427-4
epub ISBN 978-1-78191-508-0
Mobi ISBN 978-1-78191-512-7

10 9 8 7 6 5 4 3 2

Published in 2014
by
Christian Focus Publications Ltd.,
Geanies House, Fearn, Ross-shire,
Scotland, UK, IV20 1TW

www.christianfocus.com

Cover design
by
Daniel van Straaten

Printed by
Bell and Bain, Glasgow

CONTENTS

To my wife:

SUERENE RAYANNE FREEMAN

Who has walked with me down paths of suffering,
rejoicing in God's goodness all along the way.
You are my best friend. I love you.

ACKNOWLEDGMENTS

God has used various people, each in their unique calling and gifting, to aid and assist me as I've written this book. I've needed each of them. They have partnered and labored together, that God be seen in the beauty of who He is. Though they would each prefer to go unnamed, it is my humble honor to write briefly of these wonderful saints, who have been unspeakable blessings to me.

I'll never forget the morning my wife awoke to me at the computer. I had already been working for hours. Sitting her down, I informed her that the Lord had led me to start writing a book. She knew immediately what that meant; hours I'd be away from the family and she'd have the kids to herself and countless nights she'd be going to bed alone. But after reading the first few pages I had written that morning, she looked at me and said, 'This is right. This is of the Lord.' Her support has been endless and has provided me with such encouragement and strength. Words can't express the role Suerene has had as I've written this book. She is the love of my life.

Pastor Brian Williams came into my life at a time when I very much needed him. His love for the truth and uncompromising stand for the Gospel have ministered to me in very deep, personal ways. His joy in the sovereignty of God has been, for my family, a well of encouragement and hope. What an honor to call him my pastor, brother, and friend!

I didn't know when I first met Marc Testerman that he would become to me so much more then a Sunday School teacher. He is to me a friend, brother, mentor, and elder, whose council has been so valued and much needed. In matters of this book, he has spent countless hours in prayer and has been a theological springboard, who has helped me accurately communicate the truths of Christ and His promise, even in the midst of suffering.

Casey Jones has worked faithfully, hour after hour, to make it look like I can write. I can't thank her enough for all her help and support. She worked not for pay, but only for the glory of God. She is to my wife and me a sister in the Lord and true friend.

My family at Mt. Zion Baptist Church means more to me than I can put in words. They have prayed with me and believed God had purpose for such a book as this. Their covenanted fellowship is invaluable to me.

Jett Harris has been a long-time friend and brother. He challenged and encouraged me in the writing of this book, giving advice and feedback that proved to be of great value. God has used him in my life in profound and spiritual ways. For him, I am exceedingly grateful.

INTRODUCTION

Suffering is such a difficult subject to address. It's a topic that has the potential to stir our deepest emotions and remind us of past memories we had hoped to forever forget. No wonder our bookstores are filled with aisle upon aisle of the latest self-help books—books designed to teach you how to better your life, to make more money, to live a 'phenomenal' life, to have richer relationships, to get that attractive blonde to marry you in ten days ... and on and on. While some of these books may be genuinely helpful, do you see the recurring theme? We're trying, in any way we can, to avoid suffering. Write a book that will tell people how to avoid all the common heartaches and disappointments of life and, my friend, you will have a best seller. After all, this is what the world wants, what it seeks day after day: to avoid suffering at all costs. And who can blame people for wanting that?

But shouldn't it be different among Christians? Shouldn't the themes that fill the aisles at Christian bookstores convey a different message? What counsel does the Bible give about the place of suffering in the life of the believer? I fear that as Christians we have taken a human-centered approach to the concept of suffering and have lost the biblical vantage point. We've taken the bait—hook, line and sinker. We've bought into the lie of a social gospel that seeks to please self, not God. We've left our first love.

Have you ever had the thought that maybe the books that fill the Christian bookstores should differ from those lining the shelves of the secular mega-bookstores? I have. I've skimmed the titles to be found at Christian bookstores, feeling nauseous and thinking, 'Something's not right here. I mean, here's this preacher guy on the front cover of the book, smiling and pointing his finger toward me, wanting me to read a book about how to better myself, and benefit me, and promote me, and ultimately gain success for me ... But, let's face it, this book probably won't say very much that some daytime TV show host hasn't already said.' We may have a problem here. Doesn't Jesus have more to say than Dr. Phil?

The more I read the Bible, the more I'm convinced God's Word really isn't about me at all. It's about Him; it's about His glory. It's about God being praised and His fame being made known among the nations of the earth.

No one escapes suffering in this life. Yet the ways in which people respond to suffering go miles in showing who has been born again by the Spirit of God ... and who has not. The Bible is not silent on the topic of suffering, but rather brings it to the forefront as a key issue for the believer. Please understand—while life in Christ is glorious and triumphant, it can also get you thrown in jail, beaten, persecuted, rejected and scorned. Remember the accounts of Paul, Peter or others of Christ's early followers?

The book you hold in your hand may not convey what you have thought of as the common, contemporary view on suffering. Even as a book written by a believer and geared toward other Christians, the message presented in the following chapters may contain ideas that are new to you. This is not because I have had a 'new revelation' or discovered some 'new truth'. Rather, my intent is to present the revelation that was given to men of God ages ago, in timeless truth. I seek to expound upon the truths that were breathed into existence by God Himself and recorded in His infallible Holy Scriptures, the Bible.

The issue of the goodness of God in suffering forces us to take a look at what we really believe about God and His Word. Philosophy has tried to discredit the goodness of God for centuries precisely on this basis. Many ask, 'How can a God of supreme goodness and love allow His creatures to suffer?' That is the question that is addressed by this book. If we are to remain in the truths of Scripture (which we will do)—that God is all-good, all-knowing and all-powerful—then we must address the issue of suffering and its place in the plan and purpose of God.

We are unable in our natural minds to understand how a God of goodness could ever allow suffering. Yet we find in the pages of Scripture a wisdom that surpasses the wisdom of men and shows us an overarching divine plan that takes suffering, which the forces of darkness meant for evil, and uses it to accomplish the perfect plan of God here on earth. Only God could do such a thing, because only God is sovereign. It's sad that the wisdom of this world can seldom, if ever, understand the glorious mysteries of God. Yet isn't that the way Jesus said it would be?

I encourage you to prayerfully read this book and contemplate the truths herein. This isn't a perfect book, because I'm far from a perfect author. Yet if you will seek the Holy Spirit as you read (as I have sought Him as I've written), I believe He will move mightily within you and you will discover the goodness of God in suffering.

Jamie Freeman
January 2014

1

Crushed, but Not Destroyed

My Experience with the Goodness of God in Suffering

A Christian is someone who shares the sufferings of God in the world.

Dietrich Bonhoeffer

The Beginning

Her water broke around midnight. The expectant young couple scurried around with excitement, as they hopped into their car and started down the dark country road, making their way to the hospital. Their anticipation built as they arrived, elated at the prospect of seeing and holding their firstborn child. After they had checked in, they began the long wait. You could feel their excitement as they discussed their new child.

'What if it's a boy?' the young wife asked.

'It won't be a boy,' her husband replied. 'It's a girl.'

'But we need a boy's name just in case,' she insisted.

'If it's a boy, you can name him,' replied the soon-to-be father. And their joyous expectancy continued.

Around 1:00 a.m. a nurse entered the room. 'I'm going to remove the fetal monitor so you can try to get some rest,' she explained. As she left the room, the couple settled down to try and get some sleep before the real tumult began. Throughout the next five hours, not one person came into the room to check on the woman or her unborn child. Finally, at around 6:00 a.m., the nurse returned and announced that the doctor had come in unexpectedly early that day and would soon be in their room. She hurriedly repositioned the fetal monitor, then rushed out of the room without even checking any of the readings.

As promised, the doctor soon arrived. As he glanced at the monitor, panic filled his eyes.

'Something's wrong,' he said, forgetting his coolly professional manner. 'The baby is in distress. There's barely a heartbeat!' He checked and found that the child's foot had come through the cervix before dilation. Worse, the umbilical cord had wrapped around the bottom of the foot, cutting off oxygen to the baby. The doctor immediately dispatched orders to the nurses to prepare for an emergency Cesarean. As this was during the shift change, twice as many nurses were running frantically in and out of the room.

How long had the baby been without oxygen? No one knew. It had been five hours since any vitals were taken.

'What is going on?' the new mother worried, her mind flooding with fear.

The medical team quickly performed the emergency C-section, hoping to be wrong about what their training was telling them. The doctor knew that a baby could not survive more than two or three minutes without oxygen. He also knew that from the time he had first entered the room, far longer than that scant timeframe had passed. The surgery went as quickly as possible and they delivered a baby boy—a baby the deepest shade of purple a new mom had ever seen. He was lifeless, not even crying due to the lack of oxygen.

'Why did this happen to my baby?' wondered the mother behind her tears as they whisked him away to the neonatal intensive care unit. Everyone was in shock, not knowing what to think. Fear was preying on the father's mind as he chased after the herd of white medical scrubs rushing his baby boy to the intensive-care nursery.

Hope in the Midst of Pain

For the next few hours the father returned again and again to take pictures of his son through the glass to show his wife. She couldn't go and see her child yet, as her legs were still numb from the full spinal they had given her at the time of surgery. The young infant spent that day caged in an incubator, surrounded by medical professionals who were doing their best to keep him alive. It was 10:30 p.m. before the mother was able to visit her new son. It would be a week before they released her from the hospital; but her child remained there for an additional ten days.

Following her release, the young mother spent her days at the hospital rocking her baby as she sang, 'Jesus loves you, this I know ...' The young couple were beginning to have a real hope that their child would live. Maybe everything up to this point had just been a bad dream and things would soon return to normal.

However, the doctor later called them aside to speak with them concerning their child's condition. It became clear that it hadn't been just a bad dream after all. One can only imagine the flood of uncertainty that rose in their minds and hearts as they sat down to speak with the doctor. He tried to muster that calming doctor's voice as he began to explain how their son's condition could be extremely severe. He told them that their son might never walk, talk or care for himself. Though he did his best, this prognosis hit the new parents like a stiff punch in the gut. He went on to suggest that caring for the child might become overwhelming and be too much for one couple to undertake. Just as he began to offer a list of institutions where the child could be placed, the overwrought young mother interrupted him, stating with determination, 'We will care for him ourselves. No matter what it takes, we will raise our son.' That was a huge statement of faith, especially when things seemed so grim. But faith is one thing the Lord gave this couple in plentiful supply, even as they had to walk this seemingly long road of uncertainty.

The Journey of Faith

Even so, when the doctor told them that their son might never be able to walk or talk, his words must have echoed in their minds. It is news that no parent ever wants to hear. There they were, holding their new baby, and as they looked around the nursery, they saw happy, healthy babies; yet their little boy was connected to a heart monitor ... and to a future that seemed so unsure. It was an extremely difficult time for the family. Yet, they knew that God had a plan and that everything would work together for good in the end.

When at last they went home, the mother was so nervous she hyperventilated and had to breathe into a paper bag. The weeks and months that followed were filled with challenges. There were times when they would see children running and playing, and it would fill their hearts and eyes with sadness.

They worried, 'What if our son doesn't ever get to run and play? What if he doesn't have a normal childhood?' Yet, through God's grace, they fought against all the normal fears and questions that come along with such a situation.

The child was later diagnosed with cerebral palsy, a condition caused by a lack of oxygen to the brain at or around the time of birth, which results in a deficiency of muscle control that can cause impaired speech, mobility and overall muscle dexterity. He soon began physical and occupational therapy. His parents were praying and trusting that God would show His hand and, over time, He did! Their son began to make steady progress. By the age of three he was walking and talking! This was nothing short of the hand of God. Though things weren't perfect, the progress was refreshing for the family.

How Trials Turn to Gold

It's always humbling for me to tell this story, because it's my story. It was I who spent the first days of my life caged in an incubator, fighting for my life. I am that child who was diagnosed with cerebral palsy—who doctors thought might never walk or talk or care for myself. The trials that my parents and I have faced have been many, yet God has been particularly faithful to use them for His own glory.

For example, one of the first times I walked in public was on Christmas Sunday. Our church had the tradition of giving out Christmas treat sacks, and everyone would walk to the front of the church to pick up their treat. I don't know what prompted it, but I really wanted to walk up and get my own sack. So, to the amazement of our small congregation and to the glory of God, I walked up by myself, got a treat sack and went and sat in the pastor's lap. Everyone was in shock. There wasn't a dry eye in the building as our family of believers, who had stood in faith with my parents, watched as God proved Himself faithful. Needless to say, the main treat that Sunday wasn't apples and candy canes, but the demonstration of God's power as I walked to the front of the church.

As I grew older I adapted to life with my disability. My grade-school years were bittersweet. I was able to be in regular education classes with the help of a personal aid, but I was laughed at and made fun of constantly. This really hurt and affected my early childhood years. I wondered why I had to be different; thinking about it often brought me to tears. However, the laughter seemed to subside as I got older and I began to enjoy school and being around my peers. I think that age and maturity taught me how to better deal with being disabled. When kids saw that my disability wasn't a big deal to me, it suddenly wasn't a big deal to them either.

The Lord was also at work in another area of my life. Around the age of seven or eight, I became increasingly aware of my personal need for Christ to be my Savior. I really can't explain it. It was more than fleeting childhood emotions. The grace of God started dealing with my young heart in wonderfully precious ways. Though I can't recall an actual date and time when I was saved, I can most definitely recall the season of life when God saved me by His grace as I passed out of death and into glorious life. I immediately began to hunger for the things of God. On Sundays I would skip children's church so I could go into the main worship service, where I would often spend the worship hour weeping in the presence of God.

I was too young to know quite what was going on, and I certainly didn't have any theological understanding of what was taking place. But I knew God was at work. I remember having such joy in my later childhood and into my teenage years. The Lord placed in me an appetite for His Word and for prayer.

The things of God continued to exhilarate me as I experienced His presence at greater and greater intensities.

Upon completion of high school I went to college and studied theology. I had felt called to ministry since I was very young. Though I can't say why I should have been so drawn to ministry, outside of God's divine plan, it has always seemed to be a burden that God has placed on my heart. I've tried to answer that call in various ways as I've grown older; from writing short devotionals and leading teen Bible studies to starting school prayer gatherings and spending Friday nights at the mall witnessing, I've always been active in some type of ministry.

My childhood and adolescent years had plenty of ups and downs. While I thank God for all the up times, I have also learned the necessity of thanking Him for the down times as well. Those down times have been used by the Lord to teach me about His goodness in times of suffering.

Now, at the age of twenty-seven, I know that having cerebral palsy (CP) was an act of the grace of God. Anything else would have been outside the scope of divine wisdom. On the practical—yet profoundly spiritual—side, think of how CP preserved me. Psalm 116:6 says, '*The Lord preserves the simple; I was brought low, and He saved me*.'

I never dated much. Girls didn't seem to want to go out with the handicapped kid. But because of that I was saved from the hormonally-infested high school dating scene, which has led many down a dark road of sexual promiscuity and perversion, ending in guilt and shame. Similarly, I was never seduced into attending any high school parties, introduced to alcohol or induced to dabble with any types of drugs. Certainly all of this can be avoided without having to endure cerebral palsy; yet in my life I've seen the Lord use CP to preserve me and keep me in the grace of God.

Even more profound are the more spiritual ways in which God has used CP in my life. I began to seek Him earnestly at a very young age. My young spirit knew that God alone had the ability to heal me, which incited me to press into Him as hard as I could. As I grew older I began to understand that whether God healed my CP or not was in His hands; but I began to see an even greater need: to be healed of the sin-sickness we are all born with. My most pressing request of God was not that He would heal my physical body, but that He would purify all that was in me. This act of grace, known as sanctification, has been an ongoing work and is the greatest miracle anyone could ever ask for.

Beauty and Grace

God's grace upon my life has continued to amaze me, even as I've gotten older. Meeting the woman who would become my wife is one of those moments of grace I'll never forget.

I remember the first time I saw her. I was standing across the room from her, not knowing who she was; but I knew there was something special about her. I had never dated much, but there was something different about this girl.

It was time. I had to call her. I was more nervous than I had ever been. Trying to keep my hand steady, I dialed the number. I heard the phone ring, and ring, and ring again. Finally, I heard the sweetest voice. 'Hello,' she said.

'Hi Suerene, it's Jam—' I was cut off as she said, 'What? I can't hear you.' I tried harder to speak as clearly as I could. 'Hey, Suerene ...'. However, I heard, 'What? I can't understand you.' Great. It was the first time I'd tried to ask a girl out and she couldn't understand me. I thought, 'This isn't fair. Why do I have to have CP?' In my embarrassment I started to hang up the phone, but waited just long enough to hear her voice say,

'Just kidding, this is Suerene, leave me a message.' I had been wrestling with her outgoing voicemail message! I had mixed emotions at that point. I wanted to laugh. I wanted to cry. Instead I left a message asking that she call me. A few weeks later we went out together, on the first of many dates we would share. Now, six years later as I'm writing this book, we're about to celebrate seven years of marriage. It's been an amazing time. We've already made some wonderful memories; but we've also had to walk down some difficult roads together.

Suerene became pregnant almost a year into our marriage. Although it was sooner than we had expected, we were very excited. My wife had a very normal pregnancy, but at the last ultrasound we saw that our baby boy was smaller than normal. We were told that we didn't have anything to worry about. However, we would soon learn that this was not completely true.

The Day That Changed My Life
Two weeks before our due date we were walking into church when Suerene's water broke. I immediately went into Barney Fife mode, running back and forth, trying to figure out what to do. My parents were inside the church, so I went to get them. I found my mom and tried to whisper, 'Suerene's water just broke.' However, since whispering is difficult for someone with CP, I think half the church heard me. So my mom (and dad, and sister, and the lady behind them, and the pastor) followed me out into the hall. By this time Suerene (whom I had abandoned in order to take up my messenger duties) had made her way into the restroom. A nurse who attended our church came to check on her, and soon we were heading for the hospital.

Before long we had arrived at the hospital and checked in, excitedly waiting for whatever came next. It was a long wait, filled with much anticipation. Suerene had wanted a natural birth. We spent hours looking into each other's eyes as I tried to help her get through the contractions. Several hours later she decided that natural childbirth wasn't for her after all, and she would experience the wonder and bliss of God's special gift, known as an epidural. The next day at 3:20 p.m., Suerene gave birth to the most amazing 4 lb. 12 oz. baby boy I had ever seen. We were ecstatic! Suerene tried to nurse him, but it seemed he wasn't ready to eat yet.

The whole room was filled with joy. Soon we had grandparents, great grandparents and friends in the room with us. It was a festival of excitement as everyone took turns holding our new baby, Judah.

About an hour later, a nurse came in to take Judah's measurements and give him his first bath. She told us he'd be back in the room in about an hour. I grabbed our camera—time to take pictures as they measured him and gave him his bath. I was having the time of my life taking pictures of my new son. The newfound joys of parenthood were overwhelming.

However, when the nurses tried to feed him, things got complicated. Judah wouldn't take the bottle. They continued to try to feed him, and he continued not to drink. We knew then that there was a problem, and I began to panic. They asked me to leave the room, which initially angered me. If something was wrong with my boy, I wanted to be with him. However, I obliged them. After trying to feed him several more times they realized that he couldn't swallow. They would have to do some tests to find out why.

This would be the day I learned another great lesson about the goodness of God in suffering.

I had knots in the pit of my stomach as I walked down the hall. I had to tell my wife that something was wrong with our precious new baby boy. How could I tell her? What would I say? How would Suerene react?

As I opened the wide hospital door, I saw her lying peacefully in bed. Love and compassion overwhelmed me. When I finally found the words to tell Suerene about our little Judah, the fear on her face reminded me of why I didn't like hospitals. Suddenly everything seemed bleak—cold and sterile. It was as though we were going back in time to the night I was born. After the initial shock and a few tears, we began to talk. Like my parents had, we decided we were going to trust God and hope for the best.

The medical team took an X-ray to see if there was any type of blockage, but the results were unclear. The doctor explained, 'It appears that Judah has a very small opening in his esophagus. It may be due to his small size.' However, we soon learned that things weren't so simple. Judah's esophagus didn't connect with his stomach. In fact, it dead-ended. We also learned that he had an extra opening going to his trachea. This odd malformation is known as an esophageal tracheal fistula. The next day we would travel to Arkansas' Children's Hospital, where they would correct the malformations via surgery.

I was told all of this before Suerene knew it. Once again, I went back to her room and asked everyone if I could speak privately with my wife. I was tired of having to give her such news. What had seemed merely difficult before now seemed impossible. My wife had just gone through childbirth; now she had to deal with the dreadful uncertainties of the unknown.

After everyone left, I explained to her all that the doctor had told me. We sat there for several minutes and cried together. The very air seemed thick with gloom. Uncertainty can be so hard to deal with.

I remember thinking about the irony of the situation. I now sat in the same hospital I had been born in, with all the complications that had accompanied that time; but now it was my own little boy whose future was unsure. I'll admit that I had a moment in the flesh. I thought, 'You know, Lord, it doesn't seem fair. With all I've gone through in life, why do I have to go through this?' The Lord soon answered that question.

Sinai in a Waiting Room

By this time the waiting room was filled with family and friends who were waiting to hear the results of the tests that had been run that day. I went and spoke to the large group, explaining all that had transpired. Uncertainty filled the room. I could see it on so many faces. 'We're going to trust God,' I said, 'and we know He will work all things for good.' We had a time of prayer, which was very precious. Soon after that, people began to leave.

Things didn't calm down until around 11:00 that night. The whole day had been an emotional roller coaster. After everyone left, the impact of the day was weighing on my mind. It felt like a heaviness was on me; like I couldn't breathe. I knew I needed fresh air; so after everyone left, I went alone to a quiet waiting room, needing desperately to hear from the Lord. The Lord began to speak to my heart. I'll never forget what I heard ...

'It would be easy for you to say, "God, this isn't fair." Many people in your situation would say that. But I want you to know that all My ways are just; everything I do is right and true.'

I was in awe. In a moment I understood what God was saying to me, and I began to tell Him how just and right the events of the day were. Though it offends the wisdom of man and hurt my own flesh, I knew that He was in complete control. I began to tell God how right He was for allowing our baby boy to be born with such a condition, and prayed that everything would be used to glorify Christ. I left that waiting room feeling as though I were leaving Sinai, and I repeatedly told God of His justice.

How could I come to such a conclusion? That night as I sat in the waiting room, my mind was filled was a series of thoughts. First, did God know what was going to happen before it actually occurred? Yes. God, who formed and fashioned Judah in the womb, knew that Judah's esophagus didn't connect with his stomach and He knew my son had an extra opening going to his trachea. Could God have fixed it before Judah's birth? Again, the answer was obvious: Yes. I know firsthand of God's healing power. Did God choose to heal Judah and thus cure his condition? I had to be honest. No, He didn't. Judah was born with an esophageal tracheal fistula. God could have prevented it, but He did not. So, was it wise for God not to heal Judah? Yes. Everything God does, He does in supreme wisdom. Was it fair that our baby had all these problems? By grace I answered, 'Yes.' Everything God does is just. Knowing all this, I deduced that there was a reason that God, in His power and sovereignty, unfolded things the way He did. Later, that reason became quite clear.

I was in another waiting room several days later at Arkansas' Children's Hospital. I was reading in the Book of John about the blind man who was brought to Jesus. Someone asked Jesus, ' *"Rabbi, who sinned, this man or his parents, that he was born blind?" Jesus answered, "Neither this man nor his parents sinned, but* [this man was born blind so] *that the works of God should be revealed in him"* ' (John 9:2-3). Why would Jesus want the works of His Father to be manifested? The answer would come out of John chapter 17: *'Jesus spoke these words, lifted up His eyes to heaven, and said: "Father, the hour has come. Glorify Your Son, that Your Son also may glorify You"* ' (John 17:1).

Jesus wanted the works of the Father to be manifested so that the Father would receive the glory due His name. The whole reason this man had been born blind was so the Father could be glorified as Jesus healed him. This idea ran contrary to what I had learned as I grew up. I had believed that it was never God's will that someone be sick. Sickness was of the devil! You just needed to exercise your faith! Yet John's account shows that God had a specific purpose for the man's disability. He was born blind for a reason which was known only within the heart of God: that He be glorified in such a way as to bring life and hope to those who saw the miracle of healing Christ was to bring.

Satan didn't cause that man to be born blind; God did. As I pondered these things, new thoughts began to click for me. Satan didn't cause me to be born with cerebral palsy; God did. Satan didn't cause my son to have the problems he had; God did, and He did so in kindness, so that my son and Suerene and I could be used to glorify God in the unfolding of His purpose. I count all my suffering to be of the highest honor, because I see that the end purpose is the exaltation of God forever. As a Christian that is my ultimate goal; that my life glorifies Christ, in wellness or suffering. How easy it is to speak of honoring Christ when all is well. But what will we do and who will we show ourselves to be in the midnight hour, when it seems all of hell is raging against us? This is the test of true faith brought about by the Spirit of God.

As I write, Judah is six years old. What a joy he is! Judah is one of the most happy and loving kids you could ever meet. We've learned that he has a rare chromosome deletion that causes severe development delay. Judah began walking when he was three years old. He is still essentially non-verbal; though he makes some sounds and speaks a few words. His speech is affected by a condition called Oral Apraxia. While gaining full use of speech is possible for him, it will be hard-fought for. In spite of all this, the Lord is using this journey with Judah to teach Suerene and me so much about faith, trust and patience; He is fostering in us, though the trials of our son, beautiful sanctification.

My goal throughout the remainder of this book is to affirm biblically that God ordains suffering for the ultimate good of man. I encourage you as you read this book to prayerfully consider the truths found in it. God has a plan for suffering. It's a good plan that attests to His unfathomable goodness. Join me as we see the goodness of God in suffering.

2

God:
The Centerpiece of All Creation

The Goodness of God in Divine Sovereignty

*He [God] chooses what is pleasing to Himself. But that
pleasure is always His good pleasure, for God is never
pleased to will or to do anything that is evil or contrary
to His own goodness. In this we can rest, knowing that
He wishes for, and has the power to bring about, all good
things for us His children.*

R.C. Sproul

This issue of God's sovereignty is crucial to understanding the
goodness of God in suffering. Sovereignty may be defined as
'having complete authority and control over something.' The
Bible teaches us over and over again that God is sovereign over
all.

This idea of God having complete sovereignty over all things
creates a dilemma for many people. If we truly hold the view
that God is sovereign over all things, what does that mean in
the face of suffering? Many American churches teach that God

31

allows suffering, though He doesn't really 'mean for it to happen'; but since it does, '*He works all things together for good*.' This would mean that God has to react to something that was done outside of His divine will. Such theology is weak, biblically unfounded, and restricts God from being either all-powerful, in that God saw the suffering coming but was unable to stop it, or all-knowing, in that God couldn't see suffering coming from miles away.

Here's the issue. I know we want to say that God merely 'allows' suffering. It seems too difficult to say that God ever 'causes' suffering. However, if God, who is all-powerful and all-knowing, 'allows' something, His allowance is the cause.

Unfortunately, many people struggle to see God as being good, if indeed He isn't merely reacting to suffering in His goodness but is somehow serving as the cause of suffering. However, the Bible gives example after example of times when God causes His own people to suffer and, in doing so, shows His own goodness. We'll look at a couple of these examples.

God's Divine Sovereignty in the Life of Joseph

How can we even start to build a biblical perspective on suffering that highlights the absolute goodness and holiness of God while maintaining His absolute sovereignty?

Well, there are many places we could start; but just for kicks, let's go back to the story of Joseph. Now, in case you're a bit foggy on the story of Joseph, he was the son of Jacob who was sold into slavery by his older brothers, and was later thrown into a foreign prison for a crime he didn't commit. He faced years of mistreatment; but because the favor of God continued to rest on Joseph even in the midst of his suffering, he became second in command under Pharaoh. Eventually Israel faced a severe famine, which forced Joseph's brothers—the same brothers who had sold him into slavery—to seek food from Egypt. They had to go to the man whom Pharaoh had placed in charge of food storage: their brother Joseph.

Now, Joseph had grown up in the intervening years, and the things he had suffered had left their mark on him. So his brothers didn't recognize him at first. However, he recognized them. Joseph initially remained silent about the relationship, not revealing his identity. but later revealed himself to his brothers. His brothers were frightened when they realized who it was that stood before them. They remembered all too well what they had done to Joseph. Now that he was in such a prominent role of leadership, he had the ability—and the right—to take revenge. But the words that Joseph spoke to them were far from being words of vengeance, and they help us see the sovereignty of God in suffering.

Just when he was at that point where he could wreak vengeance for the wrongs that had been done to him, a place where he could seek atonement for the years that had been taken, Joseph looked to his brothers. Listen to his words.

> And Joseph said to his brothers, 'Please come near to me.' So they came near. Then he said: 'I am Joseph your brother, whom you sold into Egypt. But now, do not therefore be grieved or angry with yourselves because you sold me here; for God sent me before you to preserve life. For these two years the famine has been in the land, and there are still five years in which there will be neither plowing nor harvesting. And God sent me before you to preserve a posterity for you in the earth, and to save your lives by a great deliverance. So now it was not you who sent me here, but God; and He has made me a father to Pharaoh, and lord of all his house, and a ruler throughout all the land of Egypt.' (Gen. 45:4-8)

Joseph acknowledged that all he had gone though was from the Lord. He didn't want his brothers to grieve over what they had done; he saw the bigger picture of what God was doing. Joseph's brothers weren't the primary cause of his sufferings; God was. Yet Joseph was able to see the goodness of God in his sufferings.

God's Sovereignty in the Life of Job

Let's consider another example. The Book of Job records the tremendous sufferings Job went though. The man lost virtually everything. His children died. He lost his earthly possessions. His friends turned on him. Job himself became ill.

Have you ever considered how Job got into that mess in the first place? The first chapter of the book explains it:

> There was a man in the land of Uz, whose name was Job; and that man was blameless and upright, and one who feared God and shunned evil ...

> Now there was a day when the sons of God came to present themselves before the Lord, and Satan also came among them. And the Lord said to Satan, 'From where do you come?'

> So Satan answered the Lord and said, 'From going to and fro on the earth, and from walking back and forth on it.' Then the Lord said to Satan, 'Have you considered My servant Job, that there is none like him on the earth, a blameless and upright man, one who fears God and shuns evil?'

> So Satan answered the Lord and said, 'Does Job fear God for nothing? Have You not made a hedge around him, around his household, and around all that he has on every side? You have blessed the work of his hands, and his possessions have increased in the land. But now, stretch out Your hand and touch all that he has, and he will surely curse You to Your face!'

> And the Lord said to Satan, 'Behold, all that he has is in your power; only do not lay a hand on his person.'
>
> So Satan went out from the presence of the Lord. (Job 1:1, 6-12)

Did you notice that God, not Satan, brought up the subject of Job? It's almost as though God were baiting Satan to mess with Job. We have to say that God was the cause of Job's sufferings. He started the whole thing! Job himself identified his sufferings as being from the Lord. Speaking to his wife, Job said, *'Shall we indeed accept good from God, and shall we not accept adversity?'* (Job 2:10)

If Satan wants to harm me—and he does—he cannot do so unless God allows it. Therefore, the deciding factor in whether harm comes to me or not is God. Satan isn't the cause; he has to get permission from God, as he did with Job. The chief cause has to be God, because He has the final word.

This is one of the central points of this message. We must know that our lives truly are in His hand; it is God who brings about suffering in our lives. If He allows and thus causes the greatest calamities of our lives, nevertheless, He is good! His purposes are good! His plan is good, and He didn't bring you into the desert of affliction to harm you. He brought you there to refine and heal you. All His ways are good.

I understand the struggle to really appreciate the sovereignty of God. This is a self-effacing doctrine. It casts down the pride of man in every way. Yet in spite of this, we must continue to die to our pride. We must relinquish our lust for control and embrace God, who does things on His terms, not ours.

If you try to take a logical, humanistic approach toward understanding, you'll fail to grasp this truth. You must depend on the Holy Spirit. He will teach you. Keep in mind that this teaching is not something new. This is historically foundational

Christian doctrine. I encourage you to read the Puritans or other early church writings for further instruction in this area. Above all, read the Bible. And pray about this; even if you don't like it, pray about it.

3

Eden and the Cross

The Goodness of God in the Origins of Suffering

The person who bears and suffers evils with meekness and silence, is the sum of a Christian man.

John Wesley

The Divine Conundrum

The finite wisdom of man has always struggled to understand how suffering could exist, if indeed God was good. Philosophy has tried to belittle the goodness of God by suggesting that the very existence of suffering eliminates even the possibility of there being a God of goodness. 'For certainly,' they argue, 'a God who is all-good, all-powerful and all-knowing would never allow suffering.' Therefore, because they trust in their own finite wisdom, they fail to recognize God's infinite wisdom and the beauty of His sovereignty, as seen in the goodness of God in suffering.

We struggle to see any good coming from suffering. We cater to our flesh, looking no farther than our own immediate comfort. Anything that is difficult to understand, we reject. Anything involving personal sacrifice, we despise. So in order to justify ourselves and our weak nature, we attack the character of God based on our own selfishness.

Somehow this has been labeled 'wisdom.' But here is the problem: The finite can never understand the infinite. How could we, as mere men, expect to comprehend the wisdom of God? As God has said in times past, His ways are above and beyond our ways. Our wisdom is limited, but the wisdom of God is limitless.

> 'For My thoughts are not your thoughts,
> Nor are your ways My ways,' says the Lord.
> 'For as the heavens are higher than the earth,
> So are My ways higher than your ways,
> And My thoughts than your thoughts.' (Isa. 55:8-9)

> Let no one deceive himself. If anyone among you seems to be wise in this age, let him become a fool that he may become wise. For the wisdom of this world is foolishness with God. For it is written, 'He catches the wise in their own craftiness' ; and again, 'The Lord knows the thoughts of the wise, that they are futile.' (1 Cor. 3:18-20)

So why does God, who is all-knowing and abundant in divine goodness, allow suffering? Does He lack the power to stop it? No. He has a plan—a wonderful plan. And somehow suffering serves its own purpose in the unfolding of God's plan. To better explain, let's look back to the very origin of human suffering in the Garden of Eden.

Eden and the Cross

Eden was the birthplace of man, and of his enjoyment of the pleasures of God. Adam and Eve walked with the Lord in the garden and enjoyed all His benefits. God placed them in paradise, where they were able to commune intimately with Him. As the name would suggest, Eden (which means 'delight') was a garden of divine pleasure.

Yet something happened. As we read the Genesis account, the mood shifts. Genesis chapter two ends in a parade of innocence:

> And they were both naked, the man and his wife, and were not ashamed. (Gen. 2:25)

Yet chapter three begins on an ominous note ...

> Now the serpent was more cunning than any beast of the field which the Lord God had made. (Gen. 3:1a)

How did we move from the tranquility of creation and the innocence of Adam and Eve in chapter two to a cunning, deceptive serpent in chapter three? It seems as though things changed quite suddenly.

The word translated 'cunning' in Genesis 3:1 (or 'subtil,' KJV) is the Hebrew word *arum* which, according to Strong's Concordance, can be translated as 'prudent' in a positive connotation, or as 'crafty' in a negative connotation. We see in this verse a wise serpent, yet one who had negative motives. He was crafty. But where did this serpent come from? Let's look to Ezekiel for the answer. In chapter twenty-eight, we read:

> Moreover the word of the Lord came to me, saying, 'Son of man, take up a lamentation for the king of Tyre, and say to him, "Thus says the Lord GOD:

'"You were the seal of perfection,
Full of wisdom and perfect in beauty.
You were in Eden, the garden of God;
Every precious stone was your covering:
The sardius, topaz, and diamond, beryl, onyx, and jasper,
Sapphire, turquoise, and emerald with gold.
The workmanship of your timbrels and pipes
Was prepared for you on the day you were created.
You were the anointed cherub who covers;
I established you;
You were on the holy mountain of God;
You walked back and forth in the midst of fiery stones.
You were perfect in your ways from the day you were created,
Till iniquity was found in you.
By the abundance of your trading
You became filled with violence within,
And you sinned;
Therefore I cast you as a profane thing
Out of the mountain of God;
And I destroyed you, O covering cherub,
From the midst of the fiery stones.
Your heart was lifted up because of your beauty;
You corrupted your wisdom for the sake of your splendor;
I cast you to the ground,
I laid you before kings,
That they might gaze at you."' (Ezek. 28:11-17)

Genesis chapter three and Ezekiel chapter twenty-eight fit together like two puzzle pieces; and when we place the pieces together, it becomes easier to understand all that transpired in Eden.

The verses in Ezekiel speak of the king of Tyre. In the literal sense this most likely refers to Ethbaal, who ruled over Tyre. But this passage seems to look far beyond any earthly ruler. After all,

Ethbaal was not the *'anointed guardian cherub', 'full of wisdom, and perfect in beauty'.* This grand cherub was none other than Lucifer, the archangel who rebelled, or fell, and became known as Satan (Luke 10:18). God set Lucifer, in all his beauty, in the Garden of Eden. The text says he was a guardian. Yet, in his profane pride he tried to exalt himself and rebel against God. Because of this, God cast him out of the distinguished role of cherub, and he became a *'profane thing',* being *'cast to the ground'.*

So now when we read Genesis chapter three, we see Satan in the guise of a serpent, trying to deceive Eve. When the serpent comes to Eve, his agenda is the same as it was in Ezekiel 28: to exalt himself above God. In the Genesis account, we see him endeavoring to entice humanity into joining him as a cohort in his plan. Thus, he tempts Eve. She eats of the forbidden fruit and entices Adam to join her. When he also eats, the innocence they had shared is immediately lost. We read of this in Genesis chapter three:

> … she took of its fruit and ate. She also gave to her husband with her, and he ate. Then the eyes of both of them were opened, and they knew that they were naked; and they sewed fig leaves together and made themselves coverings. (Gen. 3:6c-7)

Sin had entered and stripped Adam and Eve of their innocence. After this initial fall occurred, they heard God walking in the garden. Although they tried to hide themselves from the One with whom they had enjoyed close communion, they soon found themselves before the Lord. They tried to explain their actions, but were without excuse. As it always does, their sin brought forth suffering.

> So the Lord God said to the serpent:
> 'Because you have done this,

You are cursed more than all cattle,
And more than every beast of the field;
On your belly you shall go,
And you shall eat dust
All the days of your life.
And I will put enmity
Between you and the woman,
And between your seed and her Seed;
He shall bruise your head,
And you shall bruise His heel.'
To the woman He said:
'I will greatly multiply your sorrow and your conception;
In pain you shall bring forth children;
Your desire shall be for your husband,
And he shall rule over you.'
Then to Adam He said, 'Because you have heeded the voice of
your wife, and have eaten from the tree of which I commanded
you, saying, "You shall not eat of it":
Cursed is the ground for your sake;
In toil you shall eat of it
All the days of your life.
Both thorns and thistles it shall bring forth for you,
And you shall eat the herb of the field.
In the sweat of your face you shall eat bread
Till you return to the ground,
For out of it you were taken;
For dust you are,
And to dust you shall return.' (Gen. 3:14-19)

Sin introduced humanity to suffering. Adam and Eve's sin not
only affected them, but it would also affect every generation to
follow. This was only the beginning of suffering, birthed by sin.

Why did God allow events in Eden to transpire as they did,
and how can we see God's goodness in the midst of them?

First, after the fall had occurred, notice the promise God made to Eve.

> And I will put enmity between you [the serpent] and the woman, and between your seed and her Seed; He shall bruise your head, and you shall bruise His heel. (Gen. 3:15)

God immediately began to speak concerning a promised Seed that would crush Satan. This Seed is Christ, who would eventually defeat Satan at the cross, and ultimately crush him on the Day of the Lord (which we will look at in detail in the final chapter). Paul speaks of this:

> And the God of peace will crush Satan under your feet shortly. (Rom. 16:20a)

God purposed in His heart before the foundation of the world that Christ would be '*the Lamb of God who takes away the sin of the world*' (John 1:29). The cross was not merely a reactionary move in response to man's fall. It was the thing that God had desired to bring about from before the world began. It was not Plan B, it was Plan A! Man's sin in the garden didn't catch God off guard. He did not have to change His original plans now that mankind had fallen. Instead, the cross of Christ was in the heart of God from the beginning of time. As A.W. Pink notes:

> To declare that the Creator's original plan has been frustrated by sin, is to dethrone God. To suggest that God was taken by surprise in Eden and that He is now attempting to remedy an unforeseen calamity, is to degrade the Most High to the level of a finite, erring mortal.[1]

---

1. A.W. Pink, *The Sovereignty of God* (Grand Rapids, MI: Baker Books, 2005), p. 20.

Why did God want things to unfold this way? Because of the glory and majesty that would be displayed at Calvary. He wanted to display His goodness. It's one thing to create and maintain a sinless utopia; it's quite another to show your willingness to go to the depths of love by sending your one and only begotten Son to ransom a bride who had been caught in sin, and to cleanse her in your own blood.

The fall of Adam and Eve set into motion the most precious display of God's goodness ever to be displayed. As Isaiah said:

> Yet it pleased the Lord to bruise Him;
> He has put Him to grief.
> When You make His soul an offering for sin,
> He shall see His seed,
> He shall prolong His days,
> And the pleasure of the Lord shall prosper in His hand.
> (Isa. 53:10)

Pleasure came to God the Father in accomplishing His plan to redeem a people back to Himself through the death and resurrection of His Son.

Genesis 3:15 allows us to understand that the cross was being preached as God's plan of redemption from the very beginning. As Matthew Henry also notes:

> A gracious promise is here made of Christ, as the deliverer of fallen man from the power of Satan. Though what was said was addressed to the serpent, yet it was said in the hearing of our first parents, who, doubtless, took the hints of grace here given them, and saw a door of hope opened to them, else the following sentence upon themselves would have overwhelmed them. Here was the dawning of the gospel day. No sooner was the wound given than the remedy was provided and revealed. Here, in the head of the book, as the word is (Heb. 10:7), in the

beginning of the Bible, it is written of Christ, that he should do the will of God. [2]

We can see the goodness of God in what transpired in Eden because it was used of God to lead us to the cross. God never desires that we sin, yet He has ordained that sin be used as part of His wonderful, purposed plan.

Foreordained, yet Condemned

This can be difficult to grasp. However, it is a truth we each much wrestle with. Did God make Adam and Eve sin? No! That would be contrary to Scripture.

> Let no one say when he is tempted, 'I am tempted by God'; for God cannot be tempted by evil, nor does He Himself tempt anyone. (James 1:13)

Adam and Eve had free agency and sinned according to their own desire. However, did God foreordain that Adam and Eve fall, knowing that by the fall He could reveal the wonders of His love as seen in the cross? Yes, He did. So, how can God foreordain such an event, yet not be morally responsible and rightly able to judge Adam and Eve for their sin?

We must understand that God's motives are always absolutely pure. He is, after all, the essence of holiness! When He ordained sin to be, He did so rightly and with the utmost purity. All of His motives were geared toward the manifestation of redemption. His intent was and is pure. How could we see the depths of His salvation if He never ordained that there be something to be saved from? If He calls forth darkness in order to show the brilliance of His everlasting light, He is good! There isn't any evil motive in Him.

---

2.   Matthew Henry, *The Comprehensive Commentary of the Holy Bible, Genesis—Judges* (Peabody, MA: Hendrickson Publishers, 1991), pp. 24-5.

Adam and Eve, however, did have an evil intent. They were not interested in revealing the glories of God, but rather their interest was in their own self-will. It was right that God judge them because their hearts were evil and their intent did not align with God's intent.

On this issue it has commonly been asked, if we believe God is sovereign over sin and thus ordains it, does that mean that God is the author of sin? For this question I recall the words of Jonathan Edwards: 'if by "the author of sin," be meant the sinner, the agent, or actor of sin, or the doer of a wicked thing; so it would be a reproach and blasphemy, to suppose God to be the author of sin. In this sense, I utterly deny God to be the author of sin;... But if by "the author of sin," is meant the permitter, or not a hinderer of sin; and at the same time, a disposer of the state of events, in such a manner, for wise, holy and most excellent ends and purposes, that sin, if it be permitted or not hindered, will most certainly and infallibly follow: I say, if this be all that is meant, by being the author of sin, I don't deny that God is the author of sin (though I dislike and reject the phrase, as that which by use and custom is apt to carry another sense), it is no reproach for the Most High to be thus the author of sin.'

Again, I know this can be very difficult to understand. I do not claim to understand it fully. However, we must know that what others mean for evil God means for good. Joseph declared as much after being sold into slavery by his brothers and put into prison: *'But as for you, you meant evil against me; but God meant it for good, in order to bring it about as it is this day, to save many people alive'* (Gen. 50:20).[3]

Though others may act with evil motive, God's purpose is always pure.

---

3. Jonathan Edwards. *The Works of Jonathan Edwards*, 26 vols. Vol. 1, 'Freedom of the Will' ed. Paul Ramsey, (Yale University Press, 1985), p. 399.

A proper understanding of the sovereignty of God is vital to the pursuit of seeing the goodness of God in suffering. In fact, I would say that if you don't understand sovereignty at some level, you cannot comprehend the goodness of God in suffering.

Therefore, it would be helpful for me to define what I mean by 'sovereignty.' Sovereignty refers to the state of having supreme authority. A sovereign nation is a nation that rules itself without any outside interference; it has total authority over itself. When I say that God is sovereign, I mean that He has total authority over all things. Nothing ever happens without the sovereign approval of God. Martin Luther gave wonderful insight into the sovereignty of God in his book, *Bondage of the Will.*

> This, therefore, is also essentially necessary and wholesome for Christians to know: That God foreknows nothing by contingency, but that He foresees, purposes, and does all things according to His immutable, eternal, and infallible will.[4]

This act of God's 'willing' the things that are—the things and truths that exist—by His own 'immutable, eternal, and infallible will' is the essence of His sovereignty. Because God is supreme and there is none above Him, then anything that exists, any fact that is true, any circumstance that arises, is only so because God, the Sovereign, allowed it.

Sovereignty, then, raises questions. How do we reconcile this truth with all the dreadful things that take place in the world? If God is sovereign over all things, why do we have holocausts, abortions and pedophiles? If God is sovereign over all things, and remains completely good, then why do things such as these exist?

Some say that God didn't plan for it to be this way; but because He gave man free will, man brought about all the

---

4.   Martin Luther, *Bondage of the Will* (Greenville, SC: Ambassador International, 2007), p. 38.

suffering. While I understand that man does have a will to do as he pleases, I do not believe that this is the sole cause of suffering (as we've seen in Scripture). Using the free will of man, who has been enslaved since Adam fell, as the sole cause of sin and suffering in this world raises all kinds of problems.

Remember that sovereignty refers to having complete control of something. Consider for a moment. Suppose that in the beginning of time God, in His sovereignty, had planned for the world to be a sinless utopia, free of any suffering. Then what would have happened when Adam and Eve sinned, and suffering entered the world? God would have lost His sovereignty and so ceased to be God. If the free will of man could triumph over the sovereign plan of God, then man's free will is sovereign, not God.

Let us also recall the words of Paul in Romans chapter eight.

> For I consider that the sufferings of this present time are not worthy to be compared with the glory which shall be revealed in us. For the earnest expectation of the creation eagerly waits for the revealing of the sons of God. For the creation was subjected to futility, **not willingly**, but because of Him who subjected it in hope; because the creation itself also will be delivered from the bondage of corruption into the glorious liberty of the children of God. (Rom. 8:18-21, emphasis added)

Paul explained that creation was subjected to futility, or suffering, not because of the will of creation, but because of '*Him*' who subjected it '*in hope*.' Who is this one who subjected creation to suffering in hope? It seems we have three options: Adam, Satan and God.

When we examine the given options, we are able to quickly weed though the first two choices. First, Adam was the created, not the Creator; therefore he cannot be the one who subjected the creation, since he is the creation.

Second, there is a key phrase in the verse that eliminates Satan from the equation—the phrase, '*in hope.*' We need to identify the hope spoken of in Romans 8:18-21. The hope in verse 20 is the coming deliverance of creation, spoken of in verse 21. Why would Satan hope for a coming deliverance from '*corruption into the glorious liberty of the children of God*'? The coming deliverance from corruption and sin is the very thing that Satan tries so hard to prevent. This is why God will eventually bring down His full wrath and judgment on Satan and the kingdom of darkness: for their opposition to the plan of God in redemption and salvation.

Therefore, the only sound conclusion is that Paul is referring to the plan of God to subject creation to suffering in order to introduce redemption and to show the glory of the age to come (that is, the new heaven and earth yet to come wherein Christ rules as supreme in ultimate peace; see Revelation 21). This coming hope brought Paul consolation in his sufferings. He knew there was a coming deliverance and that God was bringing all things to an eventual end that would be more glorious than he could possibly comprehend. Paul trusted in the unfolding plan of God. He trusted that God's plan was good!

My final case against using free will as the explanation for all suffering is that we see throughout Scripture God willfully causing suffering for a set purpose. If God didn't ordain suffering, then why did He so frequently use it to accomplish His own purposes? Over and over God used suffering in Israel to draw His people back to Him. Such is the case in the Book of Joel.

The Role of Suffering in the Days of Joel
Joel prophesied to the kingdom of Judah during a time of great calamity. The Bible makes it clear that God caused the tragedies in Judah because of the disobedience of the people. Moses had

warned Israel that their disobedience would be judged with devouring locusts that would destroy the land (Deut. 28:38-46). After they had ignored Moses' warning, his words are now painfully echoing in the ears of the inhabitants of Judah. Joel begins his prophetic call with an oblique reference to Moses' warning.

> Hear this, you elders,
> And give ear, all you inhabitants of the land!
> Has anything like this happened in your days,
> Or even in the days of your fathers?
> Tell your children about it,
> Let your children tell their children,
> And their children another generation.
> What the chewing locust left, the swarming locust has eaten;
> What the swarming locust left, the crawling locust has eaten;
> And what the crawling locust left, the consuming locust has eaten. (Joel 1:2-4)

Joel continues his message with a call to restoration.

> 'Now therefore,' says the Lord,
> 'Turn to Me with all your heart,
> With fasting, with weeping, and with mourning.'
> So rend your heart, and not your garments;
> Return to the Lord your God,
> For He is gracious and merciful,
> Slow to anger, and of great kindness;
> And He relents from doing harm. (Joel 2:12-13)

God sent plagues of locusts to destroy all Judah's vegetation and hopes of livelihood in order to draw the people to repentance. Isn't it interesting that Joel describes God in the midst of this process as *gracious and merciful, slow to anger, and of great kindness*? It was mercy that caused God to send such suffering to the land of Judah. It wasn't God being angry and venting. It was God being kind and drawing His people to repentance. Had God not sent the locusts, had God not sent the suffering to serve as a wake-up call, the inhabitants of Judah would not have experienced God's mercy in redemption. It was the kindest act God could have done. Certainly God ordained the suffering to save Judah.

Only God can decide what actions are righteous and just. Even if His deeds don't make sense to us, God rules as a Sovereign, even in the midst of suffering. His wisdom is always supreme. The primary issue here isn't whether you believe one set doctrine or another. The main issue is submission to God. How can a pot say to the potter, 'You can't do that'? If God is sovereign, then He has complete control. If God is the Potter, He will do whatever He wishes with His vessels (Rom. 9:20-21).

The goodness of God in the origin of suffering is this: that the same fall of man that gave birth to suffering also made way for the cross of Christ. Think of all the spectacular goodness that has come about because of the cross. The cross is by far the greatest display of the goodness of God that we could ever see or experience. We were redeemed from sin through the cross (1 Pet. 2:24). We were made alive with God through the cross (1 Cor. 15:22). We find peace through the cross (Isa. 53:5). The list goes on and on. Oh, the wonders of the cross! Yet had there been no fall, there would be no need for the cross, that apex of goodness and divine glory.

God's purpose as shown in the cross can never get any better. In the origin of suffering God shows Himself infinitely good by setting in motion a plan to show the greatness of His love. He introduces suffering so that later He can display His victory over it. Was it worth the fall? Was it worth years of sin and suffering in order to get to the cross? Yes! To believe otherwise is to undermine the wisdom of God and cheapen the testimony of the cross. It was well worth it.

What about your life? Know that your present sufferings, as difficult as they may be, are ordained of God for His own purpose. All His ways are right and true. Everything God does, He does in goodness. Satan will try to sow seeds of doubt in you. He'll try to make you question the goodness and sovereignty of God. But as someone who has had to suffer, let me encourage you to fully rely on God. Know that if you trust the Lord, He will cause your present sufferings to produce something more precious than gold. Have faith in God! Have faith that He does work all things together for good, for those who are called according to His purpose (Rom. 8:28). Have faith in the sovereignty of God.

4

Subjected in Hope

The Goodness of God in Sickness

*I venture to say that the greatest earthly blessing that
God can give to any of us is health, with the exception of
sickness. Sickness has frequently been of more use to the
saints of God than health has.*

Charles Spurgeon

The Opportunity of a Blind Man

The gospel of John is probably my favorite of the four gospels.
While they're all wonderful and inspired by God, I have found
myself gleaning from John the most.

John is the only gospel out of the four that is not synoptic;
its accounts differ from the other three gospels in focus and
purpose. While Matthew, Mark and Luke are more historically
biographical in their accounts of the life of Christ, John seems
to be more theological in his approach. Because his focus was
different than those of the other gospel writers, we see many

things recorded by John that we don't find in the other accounts. One such example is found in John chapter nine.

Here we read of an instance when Jesus used the healing of a blind man to show the goodness of God in the midst of sickness. As the disciples were walking with Jesus one day, they passed by a man who was blind. They asked Jesus, 'Rabbi, who sinned, this man or his parents, that he was born blind?' Jesus' reply to the disciples' question has always intrigued me. He answered, *'Neither this man nor his parents sinned, but that the works of God should be revealed in him.'* Jesus then healed the man of his blindness.

Jesus taught that the whole reason the man was born blind was so the works of God could be manifested. Before this man was ever born, God decreed that he would be blind for the purpose of the glory that would be given to God on the day Jesus passed by and healed him.

Human logic would say that it would have been better had the man been born with sight. But God had a bigger plan. Think of the power and the glory of God those around were able to see that day as Jesus healed the man born blind. Imagine all the people whose lives were changed by what they saw Christ do. It wasn't sin that made the man blind. God had a plan for the sickness.

Divine healing is one way in which God shows His goodness in the midst of sickness. Throughout the gospels we see pictures of Jesus healing the sick.

> And Jesus went about all Galilee, teaching in their synagogues, preaching the gospel of the kingdom, and healing all kinds of sickness and all kinds of disease among the people. (Matt. 4:23)

> When evening had come, they brought to Him many who were demon-possessed. And He cast out the spirits with a word, and healed all who were sick ... (Matt. 8:16)

> Then He healed many who were sick with various diseases ...
> (Mark 1:34a)

The Scripture references are endless. There is no room for doubt when it comes to Jesus' healing ministry. We see God's goodness in sickness when we see that He is our great Physician.

People often tend to debate and question whether Christ still heals today. I've heard it many times. 'Why don't we see more miracles today?' Or, 'Maybe the gift of healing has passed away.'

While I understand the question, I don't understand the conclusion. First of all, we do see miracles today. No, I'm not referring just to the preachers on television, but to true, authentic moves of God throughout the earth that are accompanied by signs and wonders, including healings. I hear some of you saying, 'Jamie, you have to be careful with that stuff.' I agree. Certainly there are movements that claim to be from God, but they are not. There are men who claim to be prophets, who even perform miracles, but are false. Jesus warned us of such. (see Matt. 7:22-23).

That doesn't undermine the fact that Jesus sent His twelve out with power also (Matt. 10:1). It doesn't undermine the fact that Paul lists 'gifts of healing' as a valid spiritual gift (1 Cor. 12:9). Certainly divine healing is one way in which we clearly see the goodness of God in sickness.

Outside the Box

However, I do not see divine healing as the only way God shows His goodness in the midst of sickness. While healing is always an eternal reality for the believer, we can also see other ways God uses sickness to show His goodness.

For example, look at David Brainerd. At the age of twenty, Brainerd surrendered to the ministry, but he still struggled with what he would later identify as legalism. At the age of twenty-one he had a real spiritual breakthrough and for the first time began to understand the role of grace in the life of a believer. Though he had already surrendered to ministry, he identified this encounter of grace as his true salvation experience. Brainerd later entered Yale University to train for ministry.

Although he would later be expelled from Yale, Brainerd would become one of the greatest voices and most profound missionaries (as he ministered among the Native American Indians) of not only his day, but any day since his time. In fact, the life of David Brainerd was so influential that it inspired the great theologian and his close personal friend, Jonathan Edwards, who later edited and published Brainerd's diaries.

Yet Brainerd constantly struggled with sickness. Even while he was in college he had to take a four-week break from his studies because he was so sick that he coughed up blood. Throughout his diary we read entries such as the following, written about his suffering with severe sickness.

> ...when the afternoon came, my pain increased exceedingly, so that I was obliged to betake myself to bed. The night following I was greatly distressed with pain and sickness; was sometimes almost bereaved of the exercise of reason by the extremity of pain.[1]

> Having lain in a cold sweat all night, I coughed much bloody matter this morning, and was under great disorder of body, and not a little melancholy.[2]

> Exercised with a violent cough, and a considerable fever. I had no appetite to any kind of food; and frequently brought up what I ate, as soon as it was down; and oftentimes had little

---

1.   Jonathan Edwards, *The Life and Diary of David Brainerd* (Peabody, MA: Hendrickson Publishers, 2006), p. 125.

2.   ibid., p. 209.

rest in my bed by reason of pains in my breast and back. I was
able, however, to ride over to my people about two miles every
day, and take some care of those who were then at work upon
a small house for me to reside in amongst the Indians.[3]

Brainerd suffered with sickness to the extent that he died of
tuberculosis at the age of twenty-nine. God could have healed his
sickness in this life, yet He chose not to. Instead, we see a different
demonstration of the goodness of God in sickness. We see the
strength and grace of God poured over Brainerd in the midst of
his illness. We see a God-given passion and determination to
preach the gospel, no matter the cost. We see a divine love for
others that caused Brainerd to elevate others above himself. As
we read about Brainerd's life, we see that he persevered through
the hardship because his heart was that the gospel be spread
abroad for the salvation of many and the exaltation of Christ.
This was of more value for Brainerd than momentary comfort
in affliction. Brainerd reveled in the glory of God, not only in
his life of sickness but, as we'll see in the next chapter, also in his
death.

What we see in Brainerd is the same type of sacrificial
selflessness we see in the Christ, whose nature was manifested
through Brainerd's sickness. Christ's words in John 15:13 are
clearly seen. *'Greater love has no one than this, than to lay
down one's life for his friends.'*

This understanding and experience may not be gratifying to our
flesh, but the outcome of Brainerd's sickness is equally as precious, if
not more so, as if he had been given a divine healing. We have to be
able to see through spiritual eyes to the point that we're able to see
God's goodness in our sufferings, even when His goodness doesn't
manifest itself the way we thought (or hoped) it should.

---

3.   Edwards, *The Life and Diary of David Brainerd*, p. 220.

In my own life I can see ways other than divine healing in which God is glorified in my sickness. I continue to pray that God would be glorified through my having cerebral palsy. Maybe this will be accomplished by divine healing, but maybe not. In the meantime, God is glorified through the steadfastness of my faith in the midst of sickness. God is glorified each time I acknowledge Him as the Healer, even if I haven't seen that healing in its full measure. God is glorified as I put all my trust in Him in the midst of my weakness. God is glorified as He becomes my strength in sickness. God is glorified when my beliefs about Him are based on His Word, and not my own experience. The list could continue. The point is that there are many ways for God to be glorified in sickness. May it be said of us that we loved the glory of God more than we loved our own comfort and wellness.

The Love That Waits to Heal

When I think of biblical examples of times when Jesus went outside of the box to show God's goodness in sickness, my first thought is of Lazarus. It's a very familiar story. Jesus' friend Lazarus is sick, so his sisters send for Him. Let's reacquaint ourselves with this passage.

> Now a certain man was sick, Lazarus of Bethany, the town of Mary and her sister Martha. It was that Mary who anointed the Lord with fragrant oil and wiped His feet with her hair, whose brother Lazarus was sick. Therefore the sisters sent to Him, saying, 'Lord, behold, he whom You love is sick.'

> When Jesus heard that, He said, 'This sickness is not unto death, but for the glory of God, that the Son of God may be glorified through it.' (John 11:1-4)

Lazarus was a devoted follower of Christ. It wasn't a lack of faith that caused him to get sick. Rather, we see that God had ordained this sickness with a set purpose in mind. Jesus makes this clear when He says, '*This sickness is not unto death, but for the glory of God, that the Son of God may be glorified through it.*' What a statement! It blows most contemporary church teaching on sickness out of the water, and puts into focus the sovereignty of God. When Jesus heard about Lazarus' sickness He wasn't at all surprised, but understood the purpose behind the sickness—that it was for the glory of God.

We get a glimpse into the goodness of God in sickness as we study Jesus' response to Lazarus' sickness. We read that when Jesus found out that Lazarus was sick, He waited a few days before going to Lazarus. In fact, it was out of His love for Lazarus and his sisters that He waited.

> Now Jesus loved Martha and her sister and Lazarus. So, when He heard that he was sick, He stayed two more days in the place where He was. (John 11:5-6)

Human logic would say that if Jesus loved the family, He would have left immediately. So why was it loving, if Lazarus was truly sick, for Jesus to wait a few days before He went to them?

When Jesus finally arrived, Lazarus had been dead for several days. Mary and Martha were in anguish over the death of their brother and the absence of Jesus. When Jesus arrived Martha began to question Him, saying, '*Lord, if You had been here, my brother would not have died*' (v. 21). But Jesus showed His wisdom and the impeccability of His timing as He displayed the glory of God by raising Lazarus from the dead. Jesus specifically pointed to these actions in order to the show the glory of God.

> Jesus said to her, 'Did I not say to you that if you would believe you would see the glory of God?' Then they took away the stone from the place where the dead man was lying. And Jesus

lifted up His eyes and said, 'Father, I thank You that You have heard Me. And I know that You always hear Me, but because of the people who are standing by I said this, that they may believe that You sent Me.' Now when He had said these things, He cried with a loud voice, 'Lazarus, come forth!' And he who had died came out bound hand and foot with graveclothes, and his face was wrapped with a cloth. Jesus said to them, 'Loose him, and let him go.' (John 11:40-44)

With one vigorous command, Lazarus arose from the dead. This glory was evident not only to Mary and Martha, but to others who were with them as well. One of the greatest testimonies that came out of this event is found in verse 45:

Then many of the Jews who had come to Mary, and had seen the things Jesus did, believed in Him.

Isn't it like God to take something like sickness, illness and even death, and use it to lead others to Christ? The whole event had a precise purpose in the wisdom of God. It wasn't an unplanned reaction on Jesus' behalf, but a perfect example of the sovereignty of God. He took suffering and made it bow to His end goal.

Jesus loved Lazarus and his sisters and knew what would be best for them. In this case, it was to see the glory of God as Jesus raised Lazarus from the dead—not merely healing him of his sickness. Jesus knew the spiritual benefit that both his friends and others who would witness the miracle would receive from seeing that type of display of the power and glory of God. Therefore, '*when He heard that he was sick, He stayed two more days in the place where He was.*'

An Earnest Expectation
One function of illness is to help us to trust God more. Consider what Paul told the Corinthians.

> For we do not want you to be ignorant, brethren, of our
> trouble which came to us in Asia: that we were burdened
> beyond measure, above strength, so that we despaired even
> of life. Yes, we had the sentence of death in ourselves, that we
> should not trust in ourselves but in God who raises the dead
> ... (2 Cor. 1:8-9)

We don't know exactly what that trouble in Asia was. But we do
know that it made Paul and those with him weak to the point
of despairing for their own lives. Yet in this circumstance, Paul
says, they learned to trust in the Lord, rather than in themselves.

What if we could learn that lesson today and stop relying on
our own flesh? What if, finally, we would truly and honestly put
all of our trust in Him? And what if sickness is the means God
uses to do this in us? Isn't that good?

Maybe your healing will be manifested in this life. If so, praise
God! But if not, does that not make you long even more for the
age to come? Could it be that God would use sickness, or some
other type of suffering, to create in us an earnest expectation for
the age to come? I think it's safe to make this assumption, based
on Romans chapter eight.

> For I consider that the sufferings of this present time are not
> worthy to be compared with the glory which shall be revealed
> in us. For the earnest expectation of the creation eagerly waits
> for the revealing of the sons of God. For the creation was
> subjected to futility, not willingly, but because of Him who
> subjected it in hope; because the creation itself also will be
> delivered from the bondage of corruption into the glorious
> liberty of the children of God. For we know that the whole
> creation groans and labors with birth pangs together until now.
> Not only that, but we also who have the firstfruits of the Spirit,
> even we ourselves groan within ourselves, eagerly waiting for
> the adoption, the redemption of our body. (Rom. 8:18-23)

Creation itself suffers under the futility caused by sin. Yet this suffering causes an earnest expectation, a looking forward to the age to come when the sons of God will be revealed.

What is this 'age to come?' It speaks of our future, eternal reign with Christ. In that day we will be fully redeemed in our body, soul and spirit. We will once again enjoy the intimacy with God that was lost at the fall. He will be our God and we will be His people. John speaks of this coming age in Revelation.

> Now I saw a new heaven and a new earth, for the first heaven and the first earth had passed away. Also there was no more sea. Then I, John, saw the holy city, New Jerusalem, coming down out of heaven from God, prepared as a bride adorned for her husband. And I heard a loud voice from heaven saying, 'Behold, the tabernacle of God is with men, and He will dwell with them, and they shall be His people. God Himself will be with them and be their God. And God will wipe away every tear from their eyes; there shall be no more death, nor sorrow, nor crying. There shall be no more pain, for the former things have passed away.' (Rev. 21:1-4)

We as believers have this earnest expectation. Although we have the firstfruits of the Spirit now, we long for the day when we are fully united with Christ. We have a heartfelt longing as children of God, even groaning for the full manifestation of the realities of the age to come. These realities should excite the true believer and fill him with expectation as we await our Savior.

The church is a betrothed bride who longs to join her Bridegroom. He has spoken His love for us, and at the appointed time we will join Him. All things will be made well. He will wipe every tear from our eyes. He will remove death, sorrow and all pain.

I believe this is one major way in which God uses sickness for good: It stirs up longings within us for the age to come. It causes me to yearn even more for Christ's return. If I'm never reminded of this life's futility and of the majesty of the age to come, then I may be tempted to become content with this age. But as I am reminded of this life's futility, it causes me to cry out as the bride, '*Come, Lord Jesus!*' (Rev. 22:20)

Trust God in your sickness. Lean on Him to meet your every need. He will show Himself faithful. He will show Himself good.

5

Judgment and Mercy

The Goodness of God in Death

*We want to reach the kingdom of God, but we don't want
to travel by way of death. And yet there stands Necessity
saying: 'This way, please.' Do not hesitate, man, to go this
way, when this is the way that God came to you.*

Augustine

Derek Rapert: His Life and God's Purpose

I vividly recall the summer of 2006. Suerene and I had just
gotten married, and my life was full of joy. Two months after we
had returned from our honeymoon, I went with our church's
youth group to summer camp.

Something very peculiar happened one night at camp:
A police officer arrived at our campsite. 'Oh no,' I thought.
'What have our kids done now?' We had a good group of kids,
though, so I wasn't really worried. Then the officer asked to

speak with whoever was in charge. The pastor stepped aside to speak with the officer in private. When he returned, his face was completely white. Obviously something was wrong. My mind began to race. I tried to talk with the pastor, but he asked me to gather all the kids and stay with them.

A sense of panic began to sweep the campsite as word got around about the officer's visit and the pastor's reaction. We knew something was wrong, but none of us knew what it could be. After we youth workers had gathered the kids into the outdoor chapel area where we were holding services, we all formed a large circle and began to pray.

Some time later I was taken aside by the youth pastor. 'Derek was killed in a car accident.' My heart melted into pieces and I began to weep.

Derek was a few years younger than I and had been a beloved member of the youth group. Everyone liked Derek. He had just graduated from high school and was planning to start college the following fall. He had everything going for him.

As kids, Derek and I were best friends. The experiences we shared together would fill a book. We were typical crazy boys and had so much fun. As we grew older, life had taken us in different directions. But when I heard what had happened, I was grieved at the loss of a good friend.

I returned home from camp on Thursday, and Derek's parents asked me to be a pallbearer for the funeral on Friday night. It was a horrifying honor. I'll never forget that evening, arriving at the funeral home for visitation. I had told myself I would be strong, and I tried to be. As we walked into the funeral home, the strong, sickly-sweet scent of lilies filled my senses. I hated that smell. It was like the smell of death; but I was calm. People greeted me at the door, hugging and showing sympathy, and still I stayed calm. But then I turned the corner and walked into the chapel. As I looked toward the front of the room I saw Derek lying in the casket, and I lost control; I mean, I really lost it. That may have been the hardest I've ever cried as an adult. I didn't mean to make a scene, but I did. It was one of the most difficult nights of my life.

Death is an extremely difficult subject. I do not take it lightly. Suffering is never an easy subject. Exploring the theme of the goodness of God isn't my frail attempt to make light of suffering. Rather, it's the only means by which we can endure suffering, maintain hope and give Christ the glory due His name. Death is a hard subject. But even in death, if we look, we can see the goodness of God.

In the death of my good friend Derek, I would have to say that one of the greatest displays of God's goodness was in the astounding, God-honoring witness of Derek's parents. His parents are both strong Christians. The grace they showed during their time of loss was unbelievable. It was supernatural. The peace of God radiated from them. In their hour of need, God abundantly supplied so much grace that it filled them and spilled out onto those around them. One of the greatest displays of God's glory that I have ever seen was shown through my friend's parents as they ministered to others through the death of their son. The character of God the Father was manifested in them. This was a large part of the goodness of God in the death of Derek Rapert.

As we look further into the goodness of God in death, we'll ponder two separate paths: the goodness of God in the death of an unbeliever, and the goodness of God in the death of a believer.

The Goodness of God in the Death of an Unbeliever

It's relatively easy to find God's goodness in the death of a believer; but what about the death of an unbeliever? Where is the goodness of God in that?

The very nature of man is hostile toward God. Paul made it clear to the Romans that no one seeks after God unless grace draws him (Rom. 3:11). We are naturally God-haters, mocking all that is good and right. We are born enemies of God because of our sinful nature, willfully at enmity with the holiness of God.

However, through Jesus Christ, God offers man reconciliation to Himself. The cross of Christ offers an invitation to come and experience forgiveness, peace ... life! Yet the majority reject this invitation, preferring the darkness of sin over the light of Christ (John 3:19). Christ draws the line and makes the call clear.

> Therefore whoever confesses Me before men, him I will also confess before My Father who is in heaven. But whoever denies Me before men, him I will also deny before My Father who is in heaven. (Matt. 10:32-33)

I cannot think of any worse outcome than to be denied by Christ before the Father. Yet the fate of those who deny the truth of Christ is clear. Paul speaks of those who do not obey the gospel of Christ and of their everlasting destruction.

> We are bound to thank God always for you, brethren, as it is fitting, because your faith grows exceedingly, and the love of every one of you all abounds toward each other, so that we ourselves boast of you among the churches of God for your patience and faith in all your persecutions and tribulations that you endure, which is manifest evidence of the righteous judgment of God, that you may be counted worthy of the kingdom of God, for which you also suffer; since it is a righteous thing with God to repay with tribulation those who trouble you, and to give you who are troubled rest with us when the Lord Jesus is revealed from heaven with His mighty angels, in flaming fire taking vengeance on those who do not know God, and on those who do not obey the gospel of our Lord Jesus

Christ. These shall be punished with everlasting destruction
from the presence of the Lord and from the glory of His power
... (2 Thess. 1:3-9)

What an interesting paradox. Those who deny the road marked
by suffering with Christ end up suffering the most, being
eternally without Christ!

I can't tell you of all the times I've debated with mistaken
believers who denied the doctrine of eternal judgment. So many
people seem to want to embrace a form of universalism that
decrees that eventually everyone ends up in heaven. 'Maybe
there is a hell,' they say, 'but people don't stay there forever. After
all, God is too good to let someone suffer like that forever.' 'They
go to hell, pay for their sin, learn their lesson, then go to be with
the Lord.' There's one huge problem with this line of thinking:
That's not what the Bible says. The Bible is clear on the doctrine
of eternal judgment. So clear, in fact, that the writer of Hebrews
lists eternal judgment as a foundational doctrine (Heb. 6:2). The
way God deals with sin is a reflection on His holiness.

I begin to see the goodness of God in the death of an
unbeliever when I take hold of the value of God's holiness and
the necessity that He eternally judges sin. God hates sin. His
hatred of sin never ceases. The minute God stops judging sin,
He also stops being holy. Consider the words of David.

> God is a just judge,
> And God is angry with the wicked every day.
> If he does not turn back,
> He will sharpen His sword;
> He bends His bow and makes it ready.
> He also prepares for Himself instruments of death;
> He makes His arrows into fiery shafts.
> Behold, the wicked brings forth iniquity;

Yes, he conceives trouble and brings forth falsehood.
He made a pit and dug it out,
And has fallen into the ditch which he made.
His trouble shall return upon his own head,
And his violent dealing shall come down on his own crown.
I will praise the Lord according to His righteousness,
And will sing praise to the name of the Lord Most High.
(Ps. 7:11-17)

David understood the justice of God in rightly dealing with the wicked. Many look at this today and think God must be cruel. David, on the other hand, looked at the judgment of God and was inspired to worship. *'I will praise the Lord according to His righteousness.'* Because God is eternally righteous, He eternally judges sin. Thus He is eternally worthy of our praise. The true child of God does not look on His judgment with disdain, but with delight.

The judgments of the Lord are true and righteous altogether.
More to be desired are they than gold,
Yea, than much fine gold;
Sweeter also than honey and the honeycomb.
Moreover by them Your servant is warned,
And in keeping them there is great reward. (Ps. 19:9b-11)

The judgments of God are entirely beneficial for the believer. The goodness of God in the death of an unbeliever is seen as God displays His righteousness and holiness in eternally judging sin.

As I see God's righteousness that eternally judges sin, I'm compelled to worship Him and to be covered in His righteousness. I am persuaded toward the fear of the Lord, that I not become the object of His holy wrath.

The death of an unbeliever serves as a sober reminder of the grace that has been shown to those who are called by His name. In myself, I am no better than he who dies in his sin. I deserve the same wrath and punishment as he. However, when I soberly contemplate the death of an unbeliever, I am reminded of the rich mercy that Christ has shown me, knowing that my salvation is entirely based on Him. Paul expounds on this thought in Romans chapter nine.

> What if God, wanting to show His wrath and to make His power known, endured with much longsuffering the vessels of wrath prepared for destruction, and that He might make known the riches of His glory on the vessels of mercy, which He had prepared beforehand for glory ... (Rom. 9:22-23)

If I had a costly gift and gave it to all, it would become common. It's like the difference between a Ford and a Porsche. If everyone drove a Porsche, Porsches wouldn't be that special. But because they're so expensive, few people drive Porsches. They have extra value. On the contrary, have you ever seen a Ford coming down the road and thought, 'Oh wow, a Ford!'? Probably not, because here in the United States a Ford is a common make of car. The salvation of God is not like a Ford. It's like a Porsche (yet infinitely more valuable). Is it unfair that not everyone drives a Porsche? No, but because they're so rare, that adds to our appreciation for them. Likewise, I am a believer chosen by mercy and grace, though I am entirely unworthy. When I see the death of the unbeliever, knowing the implications of their death and that I too deserved the same, I am filled with speechless gratitude and praise for my salvation. I too deserve the Ford, but was given the Porsche.

The Goodness of God in the Death of a Believer

The goodness of God as seen in the death of a believer is precious beyond words. The clearest expression of this goodness may be found in the doctrine of the resurrection from the dead. The writer of Hebrews refers to this doctrine, calling it a foundational truth.

> Therefore, leaving the discussion of the elementary principles of Christ, let us go on to perfection, not laying again the foundation of repentance from dead works and of faith toward God, of the doctrine of baptisms, of laying on of hands, of resurrection from the dead, and of eternal judgment. (Heb. 6:1-2)

Contained in this doctrine of the resurrection from the dead is the blessed hope of the believer. In order to fully appreciate the blessedness of this doctrine and all its implications for the believer, let's take a moment to examine it.

The doctrine of resurrection from the dead can be divided into three parts: resurrection past, resurrection present, and resurrection future.[1] All three demonstrate the goodness of God to the believer.

Resurrection Past

Herein lies the glorious truth of Christ's bodily resurrection. Christ's resurrection is the foundational cornerstone of our Christian faith. There can't be any goodness of God in death without Christ's resurrection. The Bible is impeccably clear concerning the resurrection of Christ.

> But the angel answered and said to the women, 'Do not be afraid, for I know that you seek Jesus who was crucified. He is not here; for He is risen, as He said. Come, see the place where the Lord lay.' (Matt. 28:5-6)

---

1. Thanks to my dear friend Pastor Richard Hilton, for allowing me to use his church membership booklet 'After Calvary' as a guideline for teaching on the doctrine of resurrection from the dead.

Then, as they were afraid and bowed their faces to the earth, they said to them, 'Why do you seek the living among the dead? He is not here, but is risen! Remember how He spoke to you when He was still in Galilee, saying, "The Son of Man must be delivered into the hands of sinful men, and be crucified, and the third day rise again."' (Luke 24:5-7)

For I delivered to you first of all that which I also received: that Christ died for our sins according to the Scriptures, and that He was buried, and that He rose again the third day according to the Scriptures, and that He was seen by Cephas, then by the twelve. (1 Cor. 15:3-5)

The records of Christ's resurrection are numerous, and all expound on the goodness of God as it relates to believers, both in life and death.

The first implication we see is that because of the death and resurrection of Christ, Satan, who had the power of death, is defeated.

Inasmuch then as the children have partaken of flesh and blood, He Himself likewise shared in the same, that through death He might destroy him who had the power of death, that is, the devil, and release those who through fear of death were all their lifetime subject to bondage. For indeed He does not give aid to angels, but He does give aid to the seed of Abraham. (Heb. 2:14-16)

'O Death, where is your sting?

O Hades, where is your victory?'

The sting of death is sin, and the strength of sin is the law. But thanks be to God, who gives us the victory through our Lord Jesus Christ. (1 Cor. 15:55-57)

We praise God that through the death and resurrection of Christ, we as believers have victory over Satan and death.

Christ's sacrifice is the greatest example of the goodness of God in death.

The goodness of God in the death and resurrection of Christ gives the believer justification. I know my own guilt and sin; I'm well aware that I rightfully deserve to spend eternity in hell. Yet because of the cross, Christ's resurrection and divine grace that reached to me while I was a sinner, I am justified before God and declared not guilty. As the old saying goes, to be justified means it's 'just-as-if-I'd never sinned.' The more we become aware of our own sin, the more aware we are of how wonderful this truth is.

Third, the goodness of God is seen in the death and resurrection of Christ in that it sealed Christ's claim to be the Son of God.

> [Peter said] 'Therefore let all the house of Israel know assuredly that God has made this Jesus, whom you crucified, both Lord and Christ.' (Acts 2:36)

This is the source of our confidence as believers. We can stand on the solid rock of Christ ascended and exalted, knowing that He is our great High Priest and Mediator; it is He who reconciles us to God with a better covenant, namely His covenant of salvation which was spoken first to Eve (Gen. 3:15), then later made available to all the nations of the earth through Abraham (Gen. 12:3, Rom. 4:13-16).

Resurrection Present

We know that death came into the world because of sin. However, as we have seen, Jesus gained victory over death at the cross. The manifestation of that victory as it relates to physical death will be seen fully at Christ's second coming (1 Thess. 4:13-18). However, the victory over spiritual death may be clearly seen and known now. There is a present resurrection from spiritual death that, activated by grace, leads to regeneration and salvation. Paul makes this point repeatedly.

> Therefore we were buried with Him through baptism into death, that just as Christ was raised from the dead by the glory of the Father, even so we also should walk in newness of life. (Rom. 6:4)

> And you He made alive, who were dead in trespasses and sins, in which you once walked according to the course of this world, according to the prince of the power of the air, the spirit who now works in the sons of disobedience, among whom also we all once conducted ourselves in the lusts of our flesh, fulfilling the desires of the flesh and of the mind, and were by nature children of wrath, just as the others.

> But God, who is rich in mercy, because of His great love with which He loved us, even when we were dead in trespasses, made us alive together with Christ (by grace you have been saved), and raised us up together, and made us sit together in the heavenly places in Christ Jesus. (Eph. 2:1-6)

We were born dead in sin. Yet as believers we have been made alive, resurrected by the power of Christ and brought into *'newness of life.'* Because of this resurrection we can have victory over sin. There is a life in Christ that is supernatural. His grace enables us to *'lay aside every weight, and the sin which so easily ensnares us'* (Heb. 12:1). This is how we *'perfect holiness in the fear of God'* (2 Cor. 7:1).

There is life in Christ, which brings about freedom from sin! Grace teaches us that we should deny sin and live godly in this present age (Titus 2:11-12). This is the present resurrection: that I die to my own flesh and resurrect to life in Christ. It's wonderful!

Resurrection Future

> But I do not want you to be ignorant, brethren, concerning those who have fallen asleep, lest you sorrow as others who have no hope. ... For the Lord Himself will descend from heaven with a shout, with the voice of an archangel, and with the trumpet of God. And the dead in Christ will rise first. Then we who are alive and remain shall be caught up together with them in the clouds to meet the Lord in the air. And thus we shall always be with the Lord. (1 Thess. 4:13, 16-17)

This future resurrection is another blessed hope for believers, one that solidifies the principle of the goodness of God in death for the believer. We rejoice in that past resurrection of Christ and the victory He gave us over sin, resurrecting us from our old sinful nature. But we also know that for the believer, what may seem like physical death is but 'sleeping' until Christ returns with a shout and we who sleep meet Him in the air. This is a most glorious truth! Truly death, though conceived by sin, serves as a tool in portraying the goodness of God.

> 'O Death, where is your sting?
> O Hades, where is your victory?' (1 Cor. 15:55)

For the child of God, there remains this future promise. Death will not prevail over us. We will be raised up with Christ to glorified bodies and will reign forever with Him.

The Testimony of David Brainerd

In the preceding chapter I told you about one of my heroes, David Brainerd. Brainerd was a good friend of another champion of mine, Jonathan Edwards. At the end of Brainerd's life, he was living in Edwards' home. If you'll recall, he was severely sick with tuberculosis. Edwards' daughter, Jerusha, was caring for Brainerd at this time. One day as Jerusha went to attend to Brainerd, he said to her:

'Dear Jerusha, are you willing to part with me?—I am quite willing to part with you: I am willing to part with all my friends: I am willing to part with my dear brother John, although I love him the best of any creature living: I have committed him and all my friends to God, and can leave them with God. Though, if I thought I should not see you and be happy with you in another world, I could not bear to part with you. But we shall spend a happy eternity together!'[2]

You see, Brainerd understood the glories of the future resurrection and it gave him the utmost comfort as he lay on his deathbed.

Perhaps one of the most moving parts of this story occurs a few months after Brainerd's death. You see, Jerusha, who had tended him so tirelessly, had contracted tuberculosis from taking care of Brainerd. And just a few scant months after his death, she also died of the disease. Jonathan Edwards wrote of his daughter's death:

It has pleased a holy and sovereign God to take away this my dear child by death, on the 14th of February, next following, after a short illness of five days, in the eighteenth year of her age. She was a person of much the same spirit with Mr. Brainerd. She had constantly taken care of and attended him in his sickness, for nineteen weeks before his death; devoting herself to it with great delight, because she looked on him as an eminent servant of Jesus Christ. In this time he had much conversation with her on the things of religion; and in his dying state, often expressed to us, her parents, his great satisfaction

2.   Jonathan Edwards, *The Life and Diary of David Brainerd* (Peabody, MA: Hendrickson Publishers, 2006), p. 260.

concerning her true piety, and his confidence that he should meet her in heaven: and his high opinion of her, not only as a true Christian, but a very eminent saint: one whose soul was uncommonly fed and entertained with things that appertain to the most spiritual, experimental, and distinguishing parts of religion; and one who, by the temper of her mind, was fitted to deny herself for God, and to do good, beyond any young women whatsoever that he knew of. She had manifested a heart uncommonly devoted to God, in the course of her life, many years before her death: and said on her death-bed, that 'she had not seen one minute for several years, wherein she desired to live one minute longer, for the sake of any other good in life, but doing good, living to God, and doing what might be for His glory.' [3]

In this is the essence of the goodness of God in death; that in death, God would be glorified. Indeed, God was glorified in the death of Jerusha Edwards. God was glorified as she imitated Christ in laying down her life in service to others. God was glorified as she realized that her true treasures weren't in the things of earth, but in an unseen, eternal kingdom. God was glorified as she gave her all to the purposes of Christ, even unto death.

As with everything else, death serves and bows to the will and plans of God. This is true in the death of an unbeliever that, provoking eternal judgment, serves in uplifting the eternal holiness and righteousness of God. And it is true in the death of a believer, giving way to the truths found in the resurrection of the dead. God is so very good, even in the face of death.

3.   Edwards, *The Life and Diary of David Brainerd*, p. 260.

6

The Joy of Daily Manna

The Goodness of God in Poverty

*For a hundred that can bear adversity there is hardly one
that can bear prosperity.*

Thomas Carlyle

Be Careful What You Read

I was walking through the local library when a well-known news-magazine caught my eye. On the front cover was a picture of a Rolls Royce with the caption, 'Does God Want You to Be Rich?' I thought, 'This is an article I have to read.' As I sat and read the article, a sick feeling filled my stomach. The writer discussed the increasingly popular 'prosperity gospel,' a movement with which I am all too familiar.

I was raised in churches that embraced the word of faith movement, which started in the 1970s and 80s. Much of what we know today as the 'prosperity gospel' has its roots in that movement.

It had been my aspiration since around the age of twelve to attend Rhema Bible Training Center—one of the foremost schools in the word of faith movement—after high school. However, as I grew older the Lord began to put a check in my spirit about what we were calling 'faith'. Don't misunderstand; I believe we need to embrace biblical faith; but faith for what? What is our faith to be a means toward? As I read the article in that magazine, I was deeply troubled.

The piece began with the story of a man who had lost his job in the northern U.S. He decided to move to the Houston area to attend a certain church that hosted a positive television show that had helped him in the past. The jobless man jumped at the chance to move, 'claiming' a six-figure income, a large plot of ground for a ranch, a new house and the best job available.

While these things are not wrong in and of themselves, I was shocked at the man's defining statement. He exclaimed, 'I'm dreaming big because all of heaven is dreaming big. Jesus died for our sins. That was the best gift that God could give us. But we have something else. Because I want to follow Jesus and do what He ordained, God wants to support us. It's [this church's] ministry that told me. Why would God want anything less for His children?' [1]

At this point the knots in my stomach were tightening. There were some major problems with what I had just read. First, why would anyone ever feel the need to add anything to the cross? Are forgiveness of sin and reconciliation with God not more than enough? Is that not prosperity in itself? Why would anyone

1.	David Van Biema and Jeff Chu, 'Does God Want You To Be Rich?' *Time* 168, no. 12 (September 18, 2006), pp. 48-56.

want to turn the gospel into the latest 'get rich quick' scheme? Is the gospel not more sacred than that?

Another problem was the man's next remark: 'Because I want to follow Jesus and do what He ordained, God wants to support us.' At first glace there may appear to be some truth to this statement. God '*is a rewarder of those who diligently seek Him*' (Heb. 11:6). But I don't think the reward God had in mind was a nice big SUV. I thought the rewards were spiritual, which is why Christ would say in Revelation, '*I am coming quickly, and My reward is with Me*' (Rev. 22:12).

Is there some material gain to be acquired, some earthly compensation for deciding to follow Christ? One difficulty with this is that if I say that I'm being rewarded for deciding to follow Christ, it logically follows that I'm stating that I decided to follow Christ of my own accord. My problem here is that we don't ever—nor would we—decide to follow Christ of our own accord. His Spirit draws us by His grace. I came to the cross, not of my own accord, but by God's grace and the effecting of His mercy.

Finally, did this man quote Scripture? Why should we base what we believe about God on anything outside of sound biblical truth? The man written about in the article never quoted the Bible. To what did he attribute his new revelation? To the ministry of a man, not to the Bible. Something has to be wrong when we base our beliefs on what men say and not on the Word of God.

The article went on to quote another teacher's defense of the prosperity message. She said, 'Who would want something where you're miserable, broke and ugly and you have to muddle through until you get to heaven?' Immediately certain Scriptures began to fill my mind.

He [Jesus] has no form or comeliness;
And when we see Him,
There is no beauty that we should desire Him.
He is despised and rejected by men,
A Man of sorrows and acquainted with grief. (Isa. 53:2b-3a)

The Spirit Himself bears witness with our spirit that we are children of God, and if children, then heirs—heirs of God and joint heirs with Christ, if indeed we suffer with Him, that we may also be glorified together. (Rom. 8:16-17)

In light of these passages, do we not want to share in Christ's sufferings? Yet according to the magazine article, a 'teacher of the gospel' didn't want to be a part of something if it meant suffering certain things. Yet the very description she gave of things to avoid is the prophetic, Messianic description of Jesus. Do you see the problem here?

Jesus ... Rich?

One of the staple Scriptures for the prosperity movement is found in Second Corinthians. Paul wrote:

For you know the grace of our Lord Jesus Christ, that though He was rich, yet for your sakes He became poor, that you through His poverty might become rich. (2 Cor. 8:9)

This seems clear enough. However, we need to put things into their proper context. First, if the words of Paul are inspired of God, then we know they will be in harmony with the teachings of Christ. Christ warned repeatedly about the danger of material riches.

Do not lay up for yourselves treasures on earth, where moth and rust destroy and where thieves break in and steal; but lay up for yourselves treasures in heaven, where neither moth nor rust destroys and where thieves do not break in and steal. (Matt. 6:19-20)

Then Jesus said to His disciples, 'Assuredly, I say to you that it is hard for a rich man to enter the kingdom of heaven. And again I say to you, it is easier for a camel to go through the eye of a needle than for a rich man to enter the kingdom of God. ...' (Matt. 19:23-24)

But woe to you who are rich, for you have received your consolation. (Luke 6:24)

No servant can serve two masters; for either he will hate the one and love the other, or else he will be loyal to the one and despise the other. You cannot serve God and mammon [wealth]. (Luke 16:13)

So, is Paul contending for that which Christ warned against? I don't think so. Is there a prosperity offered to believers in 2 Corinthians chapter eight? Yes. The prosperity of Christ is offered to the believer; but that kind of prosperity isn't about money. Jesus Himself said ...

Foxes have holes and birds of the air have nests, but the Son of Man has nowhere to lay His head. (Matt. 8:20)

Does that sound like financial riches to you? The prosperity of Christ rests in His intimate communion with the Father. He became poor in that He became human; He suffered, died and rose again so that we too could have fellowship with the Father. This is ultimate prosperity. To cheapen this to crass financial terms is wrong on so many levels. The magazine's author asked the pastor of the Houston church if he thought God wanted everyone to be rich. His answer, according to the article, was this: 'I think God wants us to be prosperous. I think He wants us to be happy. I think He wants us to enjoy our lives. I don't know that I'd say He wants us to be rich.'

I have a problem with this. You see, my happiness and enjoyment in life come from Christ alone, not from my financial status. I can be happy and enjoy my life without being wealthy. My happiness and joy come solely from the fellowship I have with my heavenly Father.

Please understand my heart in this. I'm not saying it's wrong to have money, and I'm not saying that God doesn't take care of His children. Certainly He does. I'm not saying that God's blessings are never financial. However, I am saying that there's something fundamentally wrong when we create ideas and doctrines that are opposed to the foundational teachings of Scripture—namely, the teachings of Christ. Christ clearly did not teach the prosperity gospel. That false 'gospel' has taken elements of truth and perverted them into something they're not.

Macedonia and the Call of Poverty

With that said, perhaps you have seen the goodness of God in financial provision. I know there have been times in my life when I have. However, I've also seen the goodness of God in poverty. This goodness can be seen throughout Scripture as well. A good place to start is in Second Corinthians chapter eight. Paul writes:

> Moreover, brethren, we make known to you the grace of God bestowed on the churches of Macedonia: that in a great trial of affliction the abundance of their joy and their deep poverty abounded in the riches of their liberality. For I bear witness that according to their ability, yes, and beyond their ability, they were freely willing, imploring us with much urgency that we would receive the gift and the fellowship of the ministering to the saints. (2 Cor. 8:1-4)

This makes no sense to the human mind. Evidently the churches in Macedonia were not teaching the prosperity gospel. If they were, it must not have been working, since the people were in deep need. Yet Paul also speaks of their abundance of joy. Isn't it interesting that the two—poverty and joy—existed simultaneously? The joy of the churches was not at all connected to their fiscal situation. Their happiness was solely in God, their joy derived from Him alone. It wasn't in what God did for them materially, or in things He gave them; no, they rejoiced in the essence of who God is. I'm happy in God, not because He'll give me a BMW, but because of the new life He has placed within me. BMWs will rust away, but the eternal joy that is found in the beauty of God will last forever. The Macedonian church remained joyful even in deep poverty because the nature of God (His holiness, love, faithfulness, kindness, grace, beauty and splendor) remained true, even in the midst of their poverty.

The Joy of Daily Bread

God may show His faithfulness in poverty by sending financial provision. Or He may show His faithfulness in poverty by the supplying of daily bread. Every day becomes a new opportunity to trust God for what you don't have, a new opportunity to see the glory of God as He once again provides something out of nothing. Imagine being the children of Israel traveling through the wilderness. Each morning you wake up not knowing where your food for the day will come from. But you remember all the times before when God was faithful to provide manna; and when He does the same thing again, you bask in the never-ending faithfulness of God. Every day is a miracle service.

Take, for example, the twentieth-century evangelist, John G. Lake. He had one of the most recognized healing ministries of the 1900s. The stories of what God accomplished through Lake are incredible. He had become very wealthy by selling insurance. He was making six figures in the early 1900s. Yet when he was called into ministry, he felt led to give it all away. The man who was once very wealthy was now penniless. However, in the midst of his poverty, God began to move. Lake's life of faith gives us some amazing stories.

In April of 1908, Lake felt a call from God to go to minister in Johannesburg, South Africa. The trip would cost $2,000, and he didn't have a cent. However, as Lake trusted the Lord, an unknown person from Monrovia, California sent Lake four $500 bills. Lake didn't know who the man was and had never even been to that city; but God provided for his need.

When Lake was ready to come ashore at Johannesburg, he needed to pay the required $125 immigration fee. Once again, he was penniless. As he stood in line, a man walked up to him and handed him a $200 traveler's check, saying, 'I feel led to give you this to help your work.' God had once again shown Lake His goodness in poverty.

The Balance of Truth

I've had times of plenty when there wasn't any question of where the next meal would come from. I've also lived in the proverbial wilderness, when each day I was able to see the hand of God move. And I can honestly testify that God has never left me hungry. He has always been faithful!

I think this is what Jesus alluded to when He said,

Therefore I say to you, do not worry about your life, what you will eat or what you will drink; nor about your body, what you will put on. Is not life more than food and the body more than clothing? Look at the birds of the air, for they neither sow nor reap nor gather into barns; yet your heavenly Father feeds them. Are you not of more value than they? (Matt. 6:25-26)

Also, consider the way in which Jesus taught us to pray: '*Give us this day our daily bread*' (Matt. 6:11). We can draw a few conclusions from these verses. First, God won't let His children go hungry. '*God shall supply all your need according to His riches in glory by Christ Jesus*' (Phil. 4:19). While He may provide in abundance, it may also be provided in increments. God may take you through a season of trusting Him daily for your bread. The goodness of God is evident in both cases.

God's goodness in poverty is also seen in the Book of Revelation. Read Jesus' words to the church in Smyrna.

> I know your works, tribulation, and poverty (but you are rich); and I know the blasphemy of those who say they are Jews and are not, but are a synagogue of Satan. (Rev. 2:9)

Jesus acknowledges the Smyrnans' poverty, but calls them rich. Why? Because He operates in a different economy than man does. According to an earthly economy, Smyrna was poor. However, they were rich in the heavenly economy in that they fellowshipped in the sufferings of Christ and thus were able to share in His rule. In the midst of their suffering He says to them, '*Be faithful until death, and I will give you the crown of life.*' (Rev. 2:10c). That is true prosperity, and it was achieved in their suffering and poverty.

Compare that to what He said to the church at Laodicea.

> So then, because you are lukewarm, and neither cold nor hot, I will vomit you out of My mouth. Because you say, 'I am rich, have become wealthy, and have need of nothing'—and do not know that you are wretched, miserable, poor, blind, and naked—I counsel you to buy from Me gold refined in the fire, that you may be rich; and white garments, that you may be clothed, that the shame of your nakedness may not be revealed; and anoint your eyes with eye salve, that you may see. As many as I love, I rebuke and chasten. Therefore be zealous and repent. (Rev. 3:16-19)

This is quite different from what was said to Smyrna, but its implications are huge. Again we see that Jesus is referring to an economy outside of man's. Laodicea was rich, but truly they were devastatingly poor and were counseled to buy this new kind of gold. This wasn't gold purchased with money; it was treasure purchased by grace. We see the same invitation issued prophetically by Isaiah: *'Come, buy and eat. Yes, come, buy wine and milk without money and without price'* (Isa. 55:1).

The call to Laodicea is timely and applicable to the American church as well. We love to look at our prosperity, but have no grasp on our spiritual bankruptcy. We don't seem to understand that we've lost our saltiness (Matt. 5:13). We seem to be blind to the fact that the world is influencing us more than we're influencing the world. We're enamored with our doctrines of prosperity, but dying due to spiritual poverty. Oh, that it not be so!

Impacting The Nations

I once went on a mission trip to Nigeria with a group of friends. We were in the south-east part of the country, in a very poor area. Most of the people there did not have electricity or running water. The water they did have was so contaminated that they were getting sick and dying from it. I had never seen poverty like this before. The people lived in small huts and had very little clothing and little to no medical care.

However, the thing that shocked me the most was that the churches in this area of Nigeria loved and taught the prosperity gospel devoutly. I couldn't understand why until I went into one pastor's home. This pastor was wealthy enough to have electricity for a few hours each day. He also had a T.V.. I remember watching American Christian television programming with him when I suddenly realized what was happening. They were trying to imitate American religion! They saw what we had, and they saw what we taught, and they thought that if they taught what we taught, they could have what we have. The problem is that this doesn't work. They had embraced a false gospel and remained in their poverty. Fortunately, we were able to meet with about one hundred pastors. We exposed the prosperity gospel, repenting on behalf of American ministers, and the Spirit of God began to fill the room as He did in Acts chapter two. It was awesome!

The goodness of God is seen in poverty as He shows His faithfulness and power in providing for our daily needs. If we love Christ, God has promised us an inheritance that is greater than anything this world could imagine. Jesus has not forgotten the poor, but holds them near His heart. He will vindicate them in righteousness.

7

Reconciled by Grace

The Goodness of God in Rejection

*It was the Lord who put into my mind (I could feel
His hand upon me) that fact that it would be possible
to sail from here to the Indies. All who heard of my
project rejected it with laughter, ridiculing me. There
is no question that the inspiration was from the Holy
Spirit, because He comforted me with rays of marvelous
inspiration from the Holy Scriptures.*

Christopher Columbus

Rejected, but Not Forgotten

Rejection is an issue that most people deal with at some point in
their life. Growing up with CP, I was always the 'odd kid'. Trust
me, I've had to deal with my fair share of rejection. However,
as time goes by I often meet others who have had to deal with
issues of rejection that reach far deeper than mine. I've spoken
with person after person who felt as though they were never
good enough. 'If he loved me, why did my father leave me?' Or,
'I thought we were in love, but she was unfaithful'. Everyone

seems to face the pain of rejection at some point in life. But God is sovereign even over this. He uses rejection, like any other trial, as a pawn in His hand. Rejection bows to the purposes of God.

Remember Joseph? The Bible says that Joseph was Israel's favorite son because he was the son of his old age (Gen. 37:3). Because of this, Joseph's brothers hated him. When the opportunity presented itself, they planned to kill him—the ultimate rejection. Finally one of Joseph's brothers, Judah, came up with a different idea. He said, '*What profit is there if we kill our brother and conceal his blood? Come and let us sell him to the Ishmaelites, and let not our hand be upon him, for he is our brother and our flesh*' (Gen. 37:26-27). So it was that his brothers sold Joseph to the Ishmaelites for twenty shekels of silver. If anyone faced rejection, it was Joseph. His own brothers hated him to the point of selling him into slavery.

The Plan of God in the Life of Joseph

The Ishmaelites who had purchased Joseph were on their way to Egypt. Once they arrived, they sold him to Potiphar, who was an officer of Pharaoh, ruler of Egypt. Because the favor of God was upon Joseph, everything he did was successful. Over time Potiphar made Joseph the overseer of his house.

One day while Joseph was attending to his duties, Potiphar's wife, who apparently had grown a little too fond of Joseph, approached him and asked him to sleep with her. Joseph refused and told her that he could not do such a thing. However, she was persistent and kept seeking to seduce him. Finally she had reached the end of her patience. Her desire for Joseph had consumed her, and she grabbed him by his coat[1] and demanded,

---

1. This wasn't a coat that was worn because of cold weather. Instead, it was a tunic, the main piece of clothing Joseph would have worn. For Potiphar's wife to have his coat in her hands was strong evidence against Joseph.

'Sleep with me!' Joseph, being a man of righteousness, ran from her—but he left his garment in her hands. Because of this, Potiphar's wife tried to turn the tables on him, crying out to the other servants and claiming that Joseph had tried to seduce her.

When word of this got to Potiphar, he had Joseph put in prison. Rejection had struck once again.

While in prison, Joseph met two men, a butler and a baker. These two had worked for the king, but had been thrown into prison alongside Joseph when they offended the king. One night the two men each dreamed a dream. Joseph found them in great despair the next morning, anxious to know the meanings of their dreams. The favor of God rested once again on Joseph so that when the servants told him their dreams, he was able to interpret them. As the men marveled at the interpretations, which they saw to be true, Joseph requested a favor of the butler in return: He asked that the butler remember him when he was released from prison. Genesis 40:23 unfolds the next blow of rejection for Joseph: *'Yet the chief butler did not remember Joseph, but forgot him.'*

Imagine being Joseph. You grow up in a home where your brothers hate you; you end up on a one-way trip to Egypt. Once you arrive there, things begin to look up for you ... until a lustful woman lies about you to her jealous husband, landing you into prison. Finally you begin to see hope, since you've gained favor with two of the king's servants—only to watch that hope evaporate as one is executed and the other forgets about your existence.

Joseph remained in that prison for two more years. He became a leader even there; but a leader in prison is still in prison. Eventually it happened that Pharaoh had a series of dreams that deeply disturbed him. He called for the magicians and wise men of Egypt, but no one could interpret his dreams.

Then something exciting happens. The purpose of God begins to unfold.

The butler recalls his time in prison, and remembers the young Hebrew man who was able to interpret dreams. He tells Pharaoh of his experience, and the ruler in turn calls for Joseph to come and interpret his dreams. Joseph is brought forth from prison, cleaned up and brought before Pharaoh. Explaining that the interpretation is not within him but is from God, Joseph listens as Pharaoh recounts the dreams. The Lord enables Joseph to interpret the dreams, and the interpretation is good in the eyes of Pharaoh. Thus Pharaoh speaks to Joseph:

> Inasmuch as God has shown you all this, there is no one as discerning and wise as you. You shall be over my house, and all my people shall be ruled according to your word; only in regard to the throne will I be greater than you. (Gen. 41:39b-40)

God had a purpose and plan for Joseph. Though he faced many difficulties, even rejection by his own family, God used all those things to bring about His ultimate purpose. Those things that appear as hindrances to us are often the very things God has ordained in order to bring about His plan.

Christ, the Rejected

Even in the life of Christ, we can see how rejection was used to accomplish God's purposes. The rejection of Christ by the Jews, which led to the cross, brought many sons to glory. Jesus knew that His rejection was for a purpose.

> And He began to teach them that the Son of Man must suffer many things, and be rejected by the elders and chief priests and scribes, and be killed, and after three days rise again. (Mark 8:31)

The Jewish people of the day had their own ideas of how their Messiah would come. Jesus didn't meet their expectations. He didn't fit into their ideology. They had built their own conception of what their Messiah would be, and Jesus didn't make the cut. They were trying to build upon what had been promised to their fathers, but they missed the foundation for what they were trying to build. Jesus was and is the Cornerstone. He is the only Messiah. Thus it was written, '*The stone which the builders rejected has become the chief cornerstone*' (Ps. 118:22, 1 Pet. 2:7).

Yet the rejection of Jesus by the Jews did not lead to devastation. To the contrary, it led to the greatest event in human history. It was the hatred and rejection of Jesus that led to our redemption!

Do you think that perhaps God had a plan in the rejection of Christ? For Gentiles it became a blessing, since Israel's rejection of Christ led to our being grafted into the body of Christ. We were offered salvation precisely because Israel rejected Christ. It's amazing to me that God would allow Israel, God's firstborn, chosen above all the nations of the earth, to reject Christ, for the benefit of unclean, swine-eating Gentiles. What did it cost God, and what did it cost Israel, for me to be saved as a Gentile? Not only did Israel reject God but, for a moment in time, God also rejected His own, Israel, that I may be saved. It fills me with such gratitude. Wow! Perhaps this is the very heart of the matter, that the goodness of God in rejection is best seen in God momentarily rejecting His own people, thus offering salvation to all who would call on His name.

Yet I don't want to make it sound as if Israel is forgotten. God is faithful to His covenant people and we long for the day when all of Israel will be saved.God's rejection of Israel was not a total rejection. Rather, it was momentary, redemptive separation. This is a huge point and one that must be understood.

The church has been shamefully ignorant for far too long on the topic of God's dealing with Israel. There remains for Israel the promise God spoke to Abraham. Again, while I am so grateful that Gentile salvation was a part of the unfolding of that plan, I also know that God never replaced the affection He had for Israel with affection for someone else. As a Gentile I am grafted into something special, but I do not replace anything. The momentary rejection of Jesus by the Jews and the grafting in of the Gentiles all serve their purpose in the unfolding of God's perfect and final plan.

Paul beautifully conveys these truths in his letter to the Romans.

> For I do not desire, brethren, that you should be ignorant of this mystery, lest you should be wise in your own opinion, that blindness in part has happened to Israel until the fullness of the Gentiles has come in. And so all Israel will be saved, as it is written: 'The Deliverer will come out of Zion, and He will turn away ungodliness from Jacob; For this is My covenant with them, when I take away their sins.' (Rom. 11:25-27)

Do you see it now? God shows His goodness to the Gentiles through turning away from Israel, yet uses His turning to promote the eventual salvation of Israel as well. Let it be known that God is good, even in rejection.

The Call to Rejection in the Life of John Bunyan

Consider John Bunyan. Born in 1628, Bunyan learned about suffering and rejection very early in life. When he was fifteen, both his mother and sister died. A year later, in the midst of that grief, he was drafted into the army. He later married; we don't know his wife's name, but she was a godly woman and within the first five years of marriage Bunyan was powerfully converted. They had four children together, the oldest of whom was blind.

Ten years into their marriage his wife died, and Bunyan was left alone with four children under the age of ten.

He soon married a godly woman named Elizabeth. By that time Bunyan was a pastor in Bedford, England.Now, the political make-up of England at the time was sketchy at best. England's Parliament tried to implement a state-run church. This had its successes and failures, depending on who was running Parliament at the time. However, in the mid-1670s, a year after marrying Elizabeth, Bunyan was sentenced to prison for preaching the gospel. To make matters worse, his newly-wed wife had just miscarried their first child. The English Parliament gave Bunyan a choice: He could either quit preaching the gospel and go free, or spend twelve years in jail. It must have been a weighty decision. In order to stand up for what was right, Bunyan would have to leave his new bride with four children, one blind, and with the emotional turmoil of having just had a miscarriage. When asked to recant and not to preach he responded:

> ... I have determined, the Almighty God being my help and shield, yet to suffer, if frail life might continue so long, even till the moss shall grow on mine eye-brows, rather than thus to violate my faith and principles. [2]

Bunyan was sent to prison, where he would spend twelve years apart from his family. He wrote, 'The parting with my Wife and poor children hath often been to me in this place as the pulling of the Flesh from my bones; and that not only because I am somewhat too fond of these great Mercies, but also because I should have often brought to my mind the many hardships, miseries and wants that my poor Family was like to meet with

---

2.   John Piper, *The Hidden Smile of God* (Wheaton, Ill.: Crossway Books, 2001), p. 56.

should I be taken from them, especially my poor blind child, who lay nearer my heart than all I had besides; O the thoughts of the hardship I thought my Blind one might go under, would break my heart to pieces.' [3]

However, God had a plan for Bunyan's time in prison. The lowly tinker would become a writer. He authored fifty-eight books in his lifetime, his most noted, of course, being *The Pilgrim's Progress*. With the exception of the Bible, *The Pilgrim's Progress* is the most widely distributed book in human history. Speaking of this masterpiece, George Whitefield said, 'It smells of the prison. It was written when the author was confined in Bedford jail. And ministers never write or preach so well as when under the cross: the Spirit of Christ and of Glory then rests upon them.'[4]

Bunyan was able to find the goodness of God in rejection and suffering, and we have had the opportunity of reaping those rewards for over three hundred years.

Rejection can take many forms. But when you face the many rejections of life, or face it because of your faith, be confident that God is in control and uses all things, even this, for His good purposes.

---

3.   John Piper, *The Hidden Smile of God*, p. 56.

4.   ibid., p. 61.

8

Perfected Strength

The Goodness of God in Human Weakness and Sin

I do not say that sin works for good to an impenitent person. No, it works for his damnation, but it works for good to them that love God ... I know you will not draw a wrong conclusion from this, either to make light of sin, or to make bold with sin ... If any of God's people should be tampering with sin, because God can turn it to good; though the Lord does not damn them, He may send them to hell in this life. He may put them into such bitter agonies and soul-convulsions, as may fill them full of horror, and make them draw nigh to despair. Let this be a flaming sword to keep them from coming near the forbidden tree.

Thomas Watson

The Humility in Carnality

There are many things that have never really been temptations for me. Alcohol has never been attractive to me. Drugs have never appealed to me. I was never a very rebellious kid and always tried to do the right thing. But as I grew up, there was one area of sin that I constantly fought.

It was the last day of eighth grade. We students were all sitting on the floor counting down the minutes until school was out for the summer. As I glanced across the room I saw a girl sitting immodestly on the floor. She was wearing very short shorts. Because of the way she was sitting, I could see up her shorts. I'll simply say that I got an eyeful. Being the sheltered, naïve boy I was, I initially turned my head. But something fired up within me. This was something I hadn't really dealt with before. I was being compelled by my newly acquired pubescent hormones. I should have kept my eyes turned away, but with that second and third look, I opened myself up to more sin than I ever would have dreamed.

Sin always starts out small. The 'hopeless' drug addict didn't get that way overnight. I left school that day, went home, and looked at as many pictures of women in bras and panties as the JC Penny catalog had to offer. But sin, if fed, never stays small. Satan is very crafty, always attempting to lead us deeper and deeper into our own iniquity. He isn't content to leave us in the shallow end of sin's pool. By the end of the summer, pictures of women in bras and panties didn't suffice. I was looking at fully nude, pornographic pictures.

This inner struggle produced tremendous guilt. I knew that what I was doing was sinful and I wanted desperately to get free. I truly loved the Lord and wanted to walk in His ways, but by this time I had gotten fairly deeply into sexual sin. I would constantly preach to myself, 'You have to be holy. You have to act righteous.' Though my plan was good, my methods for achievement were bad. I had bought into the lie of legalism that said, 'You have to act right through your own willpower.' As a teenage boy, with all my hormones, I was going to overcome lust by my own willpower?

It didn't go well for me. In fact, the more I fought in the flesh, the worse the sin became. I lost more battles than I won. With each defeat I fell more and more into shame and gave Satan more and more of a foothold. This struggle continued for quite some time.

But I'll never forget the words that God spoke to me one day. I was now a young adult. As I had been in prayer over the issue, I clearly heard, 'Flesh can't overcome flesh. Only My Spirit can overcome flesh.' These words echoed deep within me. I began to see my vain efforts of human will for what they were. Just as David killed Goliath because he fought in the Spirit of Jehovah, I too would only be able to defeat sin when I fought in His spirit, not my own. With this new understanding, I began to move in His Spirit and in the power of His might. Now, at the age of twenty-seven, I am able to say that I walk in complete freedom from sinful lust by the grace of God.

As I look back, I see how God has used the weakness of my flesh for His own purpose. Though I now enjoy wonderful freedom from sinful lust, I do so only by grace. It's not because of my strength or merit, but due to utter dependency on God. Moment by moment, day by day, I desperately cling to God as my only Source for purity and holiness. This absolute dependency produces humility. There's something very humbling in knowing you're not self-sufficient; that the only way you won't make a horrible mockery of Christ and the gospel today is by walking within the confines of grace. There's something humbling in knowing that if grace ever departed from you, as it did from King Saul, you would become as depraved as a wild animal. To put it quite frankly, the only reason any of us is Mr. (or Ms.) Sweet Christian, and not the sick sinner, is grace.

The only reason you and I don't desire adultery, fornication, murder, incest, drunkenness, witchcraft, sodomy and the like is pure grace. If left to ourselves, we would fall into at least one of these and probably more.

Understand that this is the way of sinful flesh, which we were all born with, and only Christ has the remedy. Only as Christ is strong in my weakness can I have any strength. Only in the abundance of grace and mercy can I know purity and holiness. Therefore I, like Paul, will boast in my weaknesses (2 Cor. 11:30), for by them Christ's strength is made known.

God is sovereign over temptation and human weakness. I know my sin hurts the heart of my Father, yet He uses it for a purpose. This in no way is to imply that it's all right to sin. As Paul said, *'Shall we continue in sin that grace may abound? Certainly not! How shall we who died to sin live any longer in it?'* (Rom. 6:1b-2) But in the instance that a believer does fall into an area of sin, rest assured that God will use all things for His glory.

The motivation of trying to refrain from sinning by the power of the self or will is pride. If I think I'm capable of doing what is good on my own, it's because of pride. And believe me, my pride took me to some very dark places. However, the end result was God-glorifying. In the end, I became painfully aware of the depths of human depravity, yet at the same time abundantly enthralled by the grace of God.

This is God-honoring, and herein lies the goodness of God in human weakness. Paul learned the same lesson.

> And lest I should be exalted above measure by the abundance of the revelations, a thorn in the flesh was given to me ... lest I be exalted above measure. Concerning this thing I pleaded with the Lord three times that it might depart from me. And He said to me, 'My grace is sufficient for you, for My strength is made perfect in weakness.' (2 Cor. 12:7-9a)

Perfect Strength Seen in Human Weakness

It is in our human weakness, in our sicknesses, in our temptations, in our struggles, that Christ is able to show His perfect strength. And as I see the strength of Christ, I'm able to glorify Him in it. His strength is my refuge and hope. For this reason, *'God has chosen the foolish things of the world to put to shame the wise, and God has chosen the weak things of the world to put to shame the things which are mighty'* (1 Cor. 1:27). So we know that in the successes of God's people, God will receive all the glory.

We see this in the account of Gideon and the children of Israel (see Judges chapters 6–8). Because of their sin, the Lord had delivered the sons of Israel to the oppression of the Midianites (Judg. 6:1). They began to cry out to the Lord for deliverance, and He reminded them that He had delivered them previously. They had been slaves in Egypt, and God had used Moses to lead them out of their slavery. Still, they were afraid of the Midianites and the gods of the Amorites.

Now, one of the Israelites was a young man named Gideon. Like most of his countrymen, Gideon was very fearful of what could happen under the Midianites. The Bible says the Angel of the Lord found him hiding in a winepress to thresh his wheat. He spoke to Gideon, saying, *'The Lord is with you, you mighty man of valor!'* What a statement! Gideon was hiding from the Midianites, threshing wheat inside a winepress to escape detection so the grain wouldn't be confiscated—and he was addressed as a 'mighty man of valor.'

He inquired of the Angel, *'If the Lord is with us, why has all this happened to us?'* Have you ever been at that point? If God is with me and for me, if He really cares, why are these things happening?

The Lord told Gideon to go forth, and He would help Gideon save Israel from the hand of the Midianites. With doubt still filling his heart, Gideon asked the Lord, *'O my Lord, how can I save Israel? Indeed my clan is the weakest in Manasseh, and I am the least in my father's house'* (6:15). But God had a plan. He told Gideon to gather the men of Israel.

So, after offering a sacrifice, destroying the altar of Baal and requesting the sign of the fleece, Gideon gathered together his army—thirty thousand men. It would have seemed to be a good-sized army—and needful, since the Midianites were *'as numerous as locusts'* (7:12). However, God had a different recruitment idea. He came to Gideon and said, *'The people who are with you are too many'* (7:2a). Too many? Gideon was about to go to war against a very large army, he was probably outnumbered as it was, and now the Lord was saying he had too many men to fight? Why? The Lord continued:

> The people who are with you are too many for me to give the Midianites into their hands, lest Israel claim glory for itself against Me, saying, 'My own hand has saved me'. (Judg. 7:2)

Therefore, the Lord began to pare down the number of those who fought with Gideon. The Lord told him to tell the men, *'Whoever is fearful and afraid, let him turn and depart at once.'* Twenty-two thousand men left. Gideon was left with ten thousand men to help him defeat the Midianites.

Next the Lord directed Gideon to bring his men to a watering hole. The instructions are simple, if a little odd: *'Everyone who laps from the water with his tongue, as a dog laps, you shall set apart by himself; likewise everyone who gets down on his knees to drink'* (Judg. 7:5). This test took Gideon's army from ten thousand down to three hundred.By all earthly standards, Israel had no hope of victory. How could they defeat an army as numerous as the Midianites with only three hundred men? But God had put them in that state of weakness for a purpose.

Of course, the battle did end well. The three hundred-man army of Israelites conquered the strong, trained and numerous Midianite army by the grace of God. What was impossible for men because of their lack of strength, God did in the midst of their weakness, in order to appropriate the glory due His name. This is the gist of God's goodness in human weakness.

The story hasn't changed over the past few centuries. We are still the small and untrained Gideon, battling against an enemy too powerful for us. The good news? Well, in yourself you have no hope. You have no strength. You have no remedy by which you can overcome the sin that seeks to destroy your life. Yet you do have hope! Jesus is your only hope. You haven't a prayer without Him. The good news is, He offers help. He offers freedom from sin.

In Our Sin, He Forgives

The goodness of God in human weakness and sin is also seen in His forgiveness.

> He who covers his sins will not prosper, but whoever confesses and forsakes them will have mercy. (Prov. 28:13)

There is an abundant supply of grace and mercy available to those who repent and forsake their sins.

> Bless the Lord, O my soul, and forget not all His benefits: who forgives all your iniquities, who heals all your diseases, who redeems your life from destruction ... (Ps. 103:2-4a)

If those who lived under the old covenant recognized the truths of God's forgiveness, how much more should they be seen and grasped by us who are under the new covenant?

> In Him we have redemption through His blood, the forgiveness of sins, according to the riches of His grace ... (Eph. 1:7)

The cross bears the infinite testimony of God's forgiveness toward the redeemed.

> ... having wiped out the handwriting of requirements that was against us, which was contrary to us. And he has taken it out of the way, having nailed it to the cross. (Col. 2:14)

It doesn't get any better than that! This is the goodness of God in the midst of human sin. He forgives! The sad truth is that too few Christians understand and walk in the liberty of God's forgiveness. They let past failures and sins keep them from fulfilling all that Christ has for them. I addressed the struggle I had with sexual sin earlier in this chapter. Yet there are so many who have had similar struggles who allow shame and guilt to rob them of the forgiveness and freedom God has for them. How many young people have felt God calling them to some type of ministry, but neglected to heed the call because of guilt? They bought into the lie of Satan. 'You can't serve God that way because of what you did on the computer, or with that girl (or guy).' It may even be a sin of the past, covered by the blood of Jesus, for which they've long since repented; still they let Satan the accuser rob them of the liberty of forgiveness and the joy of obedience in serving God as He has called them to serve. Don't let that be you!

Maybe for you it wasn't a sexual sin. Maybe it was something else. Whatever the case may be, please embrace Christ's forgiving power; let Him cleanse you by His blood that was shed for you. The goodness of God in our weakest hour is seen in His forgiveness and cleansing power.

Maybe you feel unworthy to be used by God. Maybe you feel unwise or unlearned. Perhaps you feel as though you've messed up too many times, or you feel too common or ordinary. I tell you, these things don't exclude you from being able to be used by God. He takes fishermen and makes them disciples. He takes God-haters and makes them apostles. He utilizes man's weaknesses in order to show His great strength. What could He do in you? Human weakness doesn't disqualify us from being used by God. Instead, God chooses to show His glory by using the weak to accomplish His purposes.

9

The Orphan, Widow and Gomer

The Goodness of God in Broken Families

Every Christian family ought to be a little church, consecrated to Christ and wholly influenced and governed by His Laws.

Jonathan Edwards

The Powerful Ordination of Family

Family was the first union God established among men. He saw that it wasn't good for man to be alone (Gen. 2:18), and therefore created Adam a helpmate and called her 'woman'. There's so much power behind God's intent for the family. There is power behind a man and his wife when they stand in agreement on the oracles and precepts of God's Word. There is power in marriages bathed in holiness, which accurately portray and testify to the coming marriage between Christ and His bride, the church.

There's power in raising children to love and fear God. The spiritual unity available within the bonds of family is one of the most powerful unions among men. The implications of what this means as it relates to the building up of the kingdom of God and the tearing down of the kingdom of darkness are endless. If one puts a thousand to flight, and two put ten thousand to flight (Deut. 32:30), then you'd better believe that all of hell is scared to death of entire families who possess the fear of the Lord and who know how to wage true spiritual warfare.

Because of this, Satan has sought to attack the spiritual unity of the family from day one. Yes, it began in the garden at the Tree of the Knowledge of Good and Evil; but it culminated with Cain when he took the life of his own brother out of jealousy. Why did Cain kill Abel? Because God accepted the offering brought by Abel, but not that brought by Cain (Gen. 4:4-5). Satan knew this family union was spiritual in nature and sought to bring division on spiritual grounds. (Have you ever wondered why your worst family fights always seem to occur on the way to church?)

Satan knows what is available within the union of a family; that is why he has tried to destroy it since its inception. It only makes sense that even today he would still be active in his mission to annihilate families so that they cease to be effective in their role as a spiritual militia, defeating the works of darkness.

The methods Satan uses to accomplish this are both endless and effective. The number of orphans in the world continues to climb. The number of fatherless homes is on the rise. Some studies show that divorce is as prevalent among confessing Christians as it is among non-Christians. Sibling rivalries and parent-child tensions continue, and the list goes on. All of these things are ploys of Satan as he seeks to render the God-given role of families ineffective and to pervert the testimony of what family represents—the kingdom of God.

As families, we should be advancing the kingdom of God by triumphing over the works of darkness; instead, too often we're like soldiers who have lost their guns, just hoping to somehow survive. It is my prayer that we would wake up, develop some backbone and prevail in the might of Jehovah; that our families would fulfill the call God has for us.

Nevertheless, we are confident that our God is sovereign, even in the midst of broken families, and that for the sake of His glory He shows His goodness in the midst of them. My goal in this chapter is to show God's goodness among the orphaned and fatherless, the strained parent-child relationships, and the marriages that seems to have no hope.

The Orphans and the Fatherless

I had a wonderful trip during the summer of 2003. I spent some time in Romania with a group from Teen Mania, doing missions work. As we began ministering in the streets, I noticed a large number of children, perhaps hundreds, who were roaming around outside. To our surprise, we learned that most of the children were orphaned and lived alone on the streets. We were invited to visit several Romanian orphanages, which were all packed full of kids with nowhere to go.

The most riveting experience I had in Romania happened as I was walking though the halls of one orphanage in particular. This wasn't a typical orphanage; it was a special orphanage that housed severely handicapped children. I'm not referring to kids who couldn't walk or were blind; these were children who were so mentally and physically disabled that they couldn't function at all without assistance.

I remember walking into one room in particular. It held about ten cribs, and lying helplessly in the beds were young children. The smell of urine filled my nose. Since this orphanage, like many in that country, was way understaffed, these little ones could be left for hours without anyone even looking in on them. Their beds were saturated in urine, as were they and their clothes. I picked up a little boy, around two years old, and began to sing to him. These kids hadn't been touched or loved in so long that they were starved for human affection. As I sang to him, 'Jesus loves the little children, all the children of the world,' my heart began to melt. He loved it. The expression on his face was priceless. I didn't want to ever put him down, but I had to. As I walked though the halls on my way out, it hit me. The Lord whispered in my heart, 'This is the kind of place the world said you would end up in, but I preserved you.' I began to cry and I understood more clearly than ever the love we saw in Jesus as He said, '*Let the little children come to Me*' (Matt. 19:14).

The atheistic humanist walks into a situation like that and asks, 'How can there be a God?' Such people are unable to grasp the hope that is found in suffering. We understand because of the knowledge of Christ; we can relate to Paul as he described our sufferings as not worthy of comparison with the glory to come (see Rom. 8:18-25). The true believer walks into such a situation and, gripped by a love that is not his own, says, 'Surely there is a God.'

I understand the severity of this issue. I understand how difficult it must be to be eight years old and never have heard the words 'I love you'; to never have experienced a bear hug from your dad, or heard your mom sing 'Jesus Loves Me' just for you. I understand that. But I also understand a love and compassion that runs deeper than any human pain. This love is referred to in the New Testament around 130 times. We know it by its Greek name, *agape. Agape* love can only come from God, and is distinctly seen in all three parts of the Godhead. The Father, Son and Holy Spirit manifest *agape* love in all that they do. It is their very essence. God is love. God is *agape*. Here we see the mystery of the one true God, who shows Himself in three Persons. God is triune in nature, yet one in love and motive. A good description of *agape* love is seen in First Corinthians chapter thirteen.

Though the pain of the orphan may be great, the love which Christ offers is greater. God has not forgotten the orphan. In fact, we can see God's mercy toward the orphan over and over in Scripture (See Exod. 22:22; Ps. 82:3; Jer. 7:6-7, 49:11; Hosea 14:3; Zech. 7:10; James 1:27). God has shown His compassion time and time again.

> Pure and undefiled religion before God and the Father is this: to visit orphans and widows in their trouble, and to keep oneself unspotted from the world. (James 1:27)

Pure religion is to care for the orphaned; it's to love orphans the way Christ loves them, and to take up their case as He did. When the rest of the world is too busy and preoccupied to show a child true love—that is, the love of Christ—it is our extreme honor to bend down and open a hand of friendship that says, 'Let me tell you about the One who will never leave you and never forsake you. When everybody else is gone and you have no mother and father, I have good news. I have really, really good news. Our God is a Father to the fatherless.' To the orphan we're able to show the insurmountable love of God.

David made this abundantly clear when he wrote, '*A father of the fatherless, a defender of widows, is God in His holy habitation*' (Ps. 68:5).

God provides a haven of refuge for the lonely. He is all-powerful and well able and willing to fill the voids in someone's life. He extends His unwavering love and compassion to the orphaned and fatherless.

The Strained Parent-Child Relationship

Parent-child relationships carry a wealth of spiritual significance. Because God portrays Himself as a Father, it stands to reason that earthly parental relationships hold a lot of weight with God. On one hand, the way I parent and care for my child shows the way I see God caring for me. I bear a testimony for my kids of what God is like as a Father. If I'm overly harsh and condemning, I give my children the false impression that God is overly harsh and condemning. However, if I'm soft and lackadaisical with sin, tolerating unrighteousness, I give my children the false impression that God is soft on sin. This couldn't be further from the truth. As a parent, I am always dependent on the leading of the Holy Spirit to guide me so that I can give a proper testimony of God the Father to my children.

Conversely, as a child I have to understand that the way I treat my parents is indicative of the way I treat God. Over and over we read admonishments in Scripture, such as this in Colossians:

> Children, obey your parents in all things, for this is well pleasing to the Lord. (Col. 3:20)

This was the first of the Ten Commandments with a promise.

> Honor your father and your mother, as the Lord your God has commanded you, that your days may be long, and that it may be well with you in the land which the Lord your God is giving you. (Deut. 5:16)

So, if I do not obey and honor my parents, I not only show a lack of respect for them, but I also show that God's Word is of little or no value to me.

We know the way things should look within a parent-child relationship. But how can we see the goodness of God amidst troubled parent-child relationships? I think our answer can be found in the Book of Malachi. Speaking prophetically of the coming of John the Baptist, Malachi declared:

> And he will turn the hearts of the fathers to the children, and the hearts of the children to their fathers, lest I come and strike the earth with a curse. (Mal. 4:6)

We know that the 'he' referred to here, prophetically called 'Elijah' in verse five, is John the Baptist (Luke 1:17). As the plan of God unfolds throughout history, leading to the coming day of the Lord (Mal. 4:1), God ordained that a man would come who had the spirit of Elijah—this was John the Baptist—and that he would turn the hearts of both fathers and children toward one another. Now, why would God decree this and make provision for it to happen? *'Lest I come and strike the earth with a curse.'* If the child remains in a rebellious state and the father continues to be disconnected from his children, this will invoke the judgment of God. Therefore God in His mercy ordained a prophet with a distinct calling and message; one who would turn the hearts of fathers and children toward each other in *agape* love. If that message would be heeded by the people, it would spare them from judgment.

God's goodness to fathers, mothers and children lies in the fact that He has given instruction as to how to maintain healthy relationships, and He has sent His spirit to turn hearts and to activate *agape* love.

The Troubled Marriage

We have looked at the spiritual significance found in the parent-child relationship. Marriage takes this spiritual implication to a whole new level. In fact, I believe marriage to be the most spiritual human relationship ordained by God.

Jesus identified Himself as the Bridegroom (Matt. 9:15). We are told that at the end of the age there will be a marriage feast for Christ and His bride (Rev. 19:9). These things are not merely symbolic, but very literal.

The Bible identifies the church as the bride of Christ. The Apostle Paul made a profound statement to the church at Ephesus.

> For this reason a man shall leave his father and mother and be joined to his wife, and the two shall become one flesh. This is a great mystery, but I speak concerning Christ and the church. (Eph. 5:31-32)

The gospel contains within it a mystery: the divine romance between Christ and His church. Therefore, it is of utmost importance that our marriages be healthy and righteous, because what God established between a man and woman in marriage is a testimony of what will be between Christ and the church. Our earthly marriages bear testimony to something far greater than ourselves.

So, we must ask, what are we to do with our troubled marriages and how can we see God's goodness in them?

Divorce, Division and the Plan of God

The American church offers a smorgasbord of teachings on the issue of divorce, many of which are not biblical. This is a topic that must be handled carefully and with reverent fear. The Bible plainly states in Malachi 2:16 that God *'hates divorce, for it covers one's garments with violence'*. Why does God hate divorce? Because it's hard on the kids? Because it makes holidays more difficult? No. God hates divorce because it perverts the testimony of Christ's faithfulness to His bride. It perverts the testimony of the God who promises to be forever faithful to His bride, the church, despite her unfaithfulness, redeeming and washing her with the water of the Word (Eph. 5:26).

Because of this, I do not believe the Bible gives allowance for divorce.[1] However, God offers great mercy and redemption for those who have been divorced. There may be those currently in a marriage that seems hopeless; if it seems that divorce is the only viable option, I encourage you that God is able and willing to take the turmoil of your marriage and bring out of it a work of redemption, to the praise and honor of His name! God can restore His testimony in your marriage. Therefore, we hold fast and believe that God is able to use the troubles and trials of the most difficult marriage, and cause them to reveal the riches of His goodness. Let's look at how He can do this.

The Unequally Yoked Marriage

There are many factors that can cause tribulation within a marriage. However, I want to focus on two issues that the Bible directly addresses: the unequally yoked marriage, and

---

1. Many will ask, 'If you don't believe there is ever biblical cause for divorce, what do you say to someone in an abusive relationship?' That's a very good question and needs to be addressed. First, let's remember God's main purpose in marriage: To bear testimony of the love Christ has for the church. Certainly, abuse is a perversion of that testimony. While I don't believe divorce is ever the godly answer, I do believe there are times when 'redemptive separation' is necessary. By 'redemptive separation' I mean that there are times when God may call someone to physically separate from their spouse for a season, with the hope and prayer that God would use that time of separation to bring about repentance and reconciliation. This may be needed in cases of abuse or in cases of repented, prolonged or unrepented sexual unfaithfulness. Such a separation must be done with much prayer and guidance from the Holy Spirit. If God does call you to separate for a season, you remain faithful to your spouse. Stay faithful spiritually, praying earnestly for their repentance and, if needed, their salvation. Stay faithful emotionally, not allowing bitterness to reside in your heart. Stay faithful sexually, not allowing any form of sexual immorality to creep in as you wait to be reunited with your spouse.

sexual unfaithfulness within marriage. How can God show His goodness in such situations?

On the issue of unequally yoked marriages, Paul wrote:

> But to the rest I, not the Lord, say: If any brother has a wife who does not believe, and she is willing to live with him, let him not divorce her. And a woman who has a husband who does not believe, if he is willing to live with her, let her not divorce him. For the unbelieving husband is sanctified by the wife, and the unbelieving wife is sanctified by the husband; otherwise your children would be unclean, but now they are holy. But if the unbeliever departs, let him depart; a brother or a sister is not under bondage in such cases. But God has called us to peace. For how do you know, O wife, whether you will save your husband? Or how do you know, O husband, whether you will save your wife? (1 Cor. 7:12-16)

Paul urges the believing spouse to stay with his or her partner, in hope that God will use the believing spouse to save the unbelieving spouse.

Here, we see the first glimpse into the goodness of God in unequally yoked marriages. Paul wrote of the sanctification of the unbelieving spouse because of the believer (v. 14).That word 'sanctified' means to be set apart. Now, please understand; this sanctification brought about by the believing spouse is not salvation. An unbeliever is not saved because their spouse is saved, neither are your children saved because you are saved. Rather, Paul was making the point that because of the godly influence of the believer in the home, the unbelieving spouse and children are 'set apart' in the sense that they are exposed to godliness. This is a gift that not everyone receives, and it attests to the goodness of God. God gives grace by exposing the unbeliever to true godliness, which may or may not lead to their salvation. This is why Paul says, *'For how do you know, O wife, whether you will save your husband? Or how do you know, O husband, whether you will save your wife?'* Love has the ability to redeem. Though human love could never cause spiritual redemption in itself, God can use the unwavering love of the believing spouse as a testimony that does lead to the salvation of the unbelieving spouse.

But what if the unbeliever isn't converted? How is the goodness of God displayed to the believer who will never be able to share in spiritual fellowship with their spouse? Certainly, spiritual fellowship is a vital part of marriage. In any healthy marriage there should be a mutual desire to follow after the things of God's Spirit, and this mutual longing will create a deeper level of fellowship between a man and his wife.

One of the most amazing things a married couple can do together in the privacy of their home is go into the depths of prayer together, or pine over God's Word together—enjoying intimacy with God together. This fuels and gives vitality to every other part of the marriage. This opens up the lines of communication and creates a new level of companionship. And, yes, this even maximizes the sexual life of married couples. But for the one who never has that spiritual fellowship within their marriage, God reveals Himself as good in that He personally provides that needed spiritual fellowship. Over and over throughout Scripture God reveals His nature by taking on the role of that which is missing in our lives. For the fatherless, He's a Father (Ps. 68:5). To the widow, He's a husband (Isa. 54:5). God Himself is able to sustain the one who lacks the spiritual fellowship intended for marriage. He is able and willing to take you to the depths of His heart. As you are obedient in being faithful to your unbelieving spouse, God will provide for you all that you need spiritually. After all, He is the Bridegroom.

But finally, what if the outcome is divorce? Where is the goodness of God then? Let's revisit the words of Paul.

> But if the unbeliever departs, let him depart; a brother or a sister is not under bondage in such cases. But God has called us to peace. (1 Cor. 7:15)

In the most trying of situations, God has called us to peace. Divorce is always painful. Yet the believer has access to ever-abiding peace in Christ. Remember the words of Christ:

> These things I have spoken to you, that in Me you may have peace. In the world you will have tribulation; but be of good cheer, I have overcome the world. (John 16:33)

Don't misunderstand me. Divorce is always a failure in relationship. There is always much to be lost. However, after you've done all you can in fighting for the marriage, if your unbelieving spouse walks away, you must rest in the grace that you are not under bondage and are called to Christ's perfect peace.

There will always be tribulation in this world. However, the Christian has this promise of peace in Christ. You remain His forever! He is your Spouse, and He promises to love you with an everlasting love (Jer. 31:3).

Hope for the Unequally Yoked Marriage

A friend who served at a ministry based in Minnesota received a letter from a man who was serving on the mission field and was having difficulties in his marriage. The problems were based on the fact that this man's wife didn't want to be on the mission field. In fact, she didn't want to be in ministry at all. My friend wrote this man a reply that was particularly anointed in its dealing with the issue of the goodness of God in the midst of an unequally yoked marriage. He refers to a mutual friend of ours, Bob (his name has been changed to protect his privacy), who struggled in a strained marriage as well. With my friend's permission, I have included the letter in this section in hope that the truths it contains will minister to you as they did me.

My heart aches in identification with what I know is more of a suffering than many can conceive. What man is it who can bear up under every new onslaught with perfect repose? Who is sufficient? But brother, isn't that the point?

I do not presume to instruct a well-instructed brother, but I remind you of what I must ever remind myself, and that is: It is not our prerogative to set limits on what we are obliged to suffer for Christ's sake. Our view of God's sovereignty in all things does not permit us that luxury. If only you could know, and perhaps you do know something, of what our brother Bob believed he was required to suffer in a marriage that I can scarce conceive was any less troubled and difficult, yea, impossible.

Bob lived with such marital opposition as few will ever imagine. He did it for the sake of covenant, not for the eyes of men, but for the instruction of angels through the things that only he and the Lord knew were being endured. Satan hates covenant, and is looking to drag it through the dirt, and God is permitting our commitment to covenant to be tested, sometimes severely.

True martyrdom is often hidden from public view; it remains nonetheless a demonstration before the angels, both fallen and elect. Our appointed sufferings do not often come in tidy, neat categories. They do not always come by overt acts of open persecution through men. It comes in many silent and hidden ways that are known and marked by God alone.

In whatever form our cross comes, we are able to say to all enemies both spiritual and physical, 'you could have no power at all unless it had been given (permitted/ordained) from above' (John 19:11). Such demonically mediated afflictions, attacks and seeming contradictions of circumstance come as a test to be seen and marked of angels, and also to grant the tried and buffeted believer the opportunity to convert any and everything into a far more exceeding weight of glory through the choice to bear whatever God is sending or permitting. Only it is important that we understand that we are not the ones who choose the form the test should take. We trust that decision to God and ease ourselves of nothing, but rather suffer in patience of faith whatever comes as His wise choice, perfectly tailored to the work He has in mind for each unique servant son and daughter.

The Scripture says, 'He that has suffered in the flesh has ceased from sin'. That doesn't only mean that our life has been crowned by an ultimate act of martyr obedience. It speaks of everyday events in which we choose suffering rather than to ease ourselves, and so serve notice to the principalities and powers that we will not bow under their fierce threats. That choice in the face of ultimate threat is the wisdom of the cross.

When we ease ourselves in a way that is not led by the Spirit, we actually capitulate and concede defeat to the powers with which God is in ongoing contention. We miss the moment. We concede another victory to the wisdom of the powers through cross avoidance.

Even the way we interpret our situation is a test of how we have been taught of God. I know that many leave marriages by a well-reasoned ethic of mercy to the other suffering partner, and of course, always, separation is deemed necessary for the sake of 'the children'. That is the rationale of humanism, i.e., what's 'best' for all concerned. But I hold with Jesus, that unless there has been the dissolution of the covenant through an act of fornication, anything short of the life-threatening peril or persistent physical abuse, all conflict between covenant partners is a call to the suffering of the cross (even if it comes as 'death by inches') for the sake of the covenant to the greater glory of God before the watching angels. Benighted man will never know and appreciate the inside story of what a child of God is enduring for Christ's sake; but it is never for his eyes anyway.

I'm speaking here of a secret that is revealed in our sufferings that, if the believer knew, there would be edification and joy in the endurance, without resentment or murmuring towards God or man. But this view requires that we see the truth of Romans 8:28 in all our sufferings, and not only those of the more 'noble' kind. We are not always victims. Sometimes we do exacerbate what we are required to endure by the self-preserving way we interpret and react to our circumstance.

In fact, it is those 'noble' kinds of sufferings that I've seen come to brothers of a Pharisaical spirit that made them much stronger in that spirit than ever before. The lesson I take is that in those times of gross injustice, we must not find anything in ourselves in which to glory. If we are keenly aware that there is nothing in us that makes us to differ (1 Cor. 4:7), and that it is only through Christ's strength that we are able to endure the test, we are able to give God all the glory for amazing grace, and thus escape spiritual pride.

No, believe me when I say, God rubbed Bob's face in it, and through it, he became a masterpiece of grace before the angels. To this day, many despise him for his failures in his marriage, and you know, he was indeed partly to blame and in many particulars at fault. Yes, he might have done better. But you know, he stuck it out; he endured. In fact, if he ever entertained not toughing it out, I believe I would have known it. Whatever poor humanity judges of that brother, in this matter, I will go to bat for him. What he endured, though not without fault, counted for something; it will count forever.

Finally, having said this, I want to underscore a critical element. I believe it is important to God that the call to 'embrace our chains', in whatever form, must never be done reluctantly or out of a pure sense of duty. Love turns duty into delight, even our sufferings, when received as from God for our increase in humility and grace.

We are not sufficient; that's true. We weren't meant to be. Yet there's a choice, and many times it is a choice that is only seen and appreciated in heaven. I am resolved to remember you in my prayers. The Lord be with your spirit.

Hope in Sexual Unfaithfulness

Sexual unfaithfulness is one of the most painful wounds that can come from marriage. Sex is so sacred, and its testimony is so profound. Remember the words of Paul.

> 'For this reason a man shall leave his father and mother and be joined to his wife, and the two shall become one flesh.' This is a great mystery, but I speak concerning Christ and the church. (Eph. 5:31-32)

Paul speaks of the two becoming one flesh, which we commonly understand to refer to sexual intercourse. This is partly true. But Paul shows us the deeper meaning, not only of this passage, but of the physical act itself. There's something profoundly spiritual, which goes far beyond the physical, that happens when a husband and wife become one during intercourse. God has ordained that sex be the physical expression by which spiritual realities are manifested. When a married couple becomes one sexually, they also become one spiritually and emotionally. Therefore, when you become unfaithful sexually, by default you've become unfaithful spiritually and emotionally and have been unfaithful to the entire covenant of marriage.

Therefore, the pain of sexual unfaithfulness isn't merely that you've sinned against your spouse physically, but that you have sinned against your spouse on every level of the marriage covenant. How can God redeem such a situation and show His goodness though it? I'm glad you asked!

First, the goodness of God is often most clearly seen by those whose spouse has been unfaithful, in that they are able to lay hold of Christ's unconditional love and forgiving power. After all, we have all been guilty of spiritual unfaithfulness to our Bridegroom, Jesus. We have all played the whore. Yet He offers us streams of abundant life.

God's grace and mercy toward us have been abundant. His forgiveness has been rich. After we went to lie with the world, He offered His hand and took us back. We deserved judgment, yet He gave mercy.

It's hard to understand the pain of being betrayed by your spouse unless you have had to walk down that dark, burdensome road. It's hard to understand the magnitude of forgiveness that would be required for such an act unless you are one of those who know the pain of being betrayed. Yet God can use that pain and hurt to show you the depths with which He loves you. As you welcome your spouse back into your home, back into your arms and back into your heart, God can teach you concerning the putting down of pride, which would seek to defend self, and the raising up of righteousness, which covers and forgives a multitude of sins.

Case in Point: Hosea

Perhaps the best example of these truths is seen in the life of the prophet Hosea. Hosea was called of God to a particularly difficult ministry. God came to him and said, '*Go, take yourself a wife of harlotry and children of harlotry*' (Hosea 1:2b).

It's not exactly what every man wants to hear: 'Hey, go marry a whore.' Yet God clearly explains Himself as He gives the call a second time.

> Then the Lord said to me, 'Go again, love a woman who is loved by a lover and is committing adultery, just like the love of the Lord for the children of Israel, who look to other gods and love the raisin cakes of the pagans.' (Hosea 3:1)

God had pronounced His love for Israel time and time again. From the time He first made a covenant with Abraham, He had shown His favor was on Israel above every other nation on earth. Through the prophets He had declared that He was betrothed to His people (Hosea 2:19). Still, the children of Israel constantly strayed and followed after other gods. Even when God was abundantly faithful to them, they remained defiantly unfaithful. But God's love and desire for Israel stood firm. Thus, He called Hosea to marry a woman, knowing beforehand that she would be unfaithful, in order to give testimony to His unconditional love for Israel.

It may seem far-fetched that I could suggest that God has a sovereign, good purpose in something as awful as a sexually unfaithful marriage. But the life of Hosea makes my case airtight. Was God good to Hosea? Of course He was. God allowed Hosea to see into the depths of His unconditional love. Hosea got to see firsthand that God's promise would remain true.

Were there times when the promise seemed sketchy, at least in the eyes of men? Yes. After all, in His anger God tells Hosea to name his second child Lo-Ruhamah (literally, 'No-Mercy'), saying, '*I will no longer have mercy on the house of Israel, but I will utterly take them away*' (Hosea 1:6). Later, when Hosea's wife had given birth to a third child, we read ...

Now when she had weaned Lo-Ruhamah, she conceived and bore a son. Then God said: 'Call his name Lo-Ammi [lit., 'Not-My-People'], for you are not My people, and I will not be your God.' (Hosea 1:8-9)

Had the promise failed? Did God divorce Israel? No. We must keep reading to see what else God said.

'I will punish her
For the days of the Baals to which she burned incense.
She decked herself with her earrings and jewelry,
And went after her lovers;
But Me she forgot,' says the Lord.
'Therefore, behold, I will allure her,
Will bring her into the wilderness,
And speak comfort to her.
I will give her her vineyards from there,
And the Valley of Achor as a door of hope;
She shall sing there,
As in the days of her youth,
As in the day when she came up from the land of Egypt.
And it shall be, in that day,' says the Lord,
'That you will call Me "My Husband,"
And no longer call me "My Master"' ... (Hosea 2:13-16)

The passage continues to God's conclusion.

I will betroth you to Me forever; yes, I will betroth you to Me in righteousness and justice, in loving-kindness and mercy; I will betroth you to me in faithfulness, and you shall know the Lord. (Hosea 2:19-20)

Israel had been unfaithful. She had gone after other gods, and God's prescription for her was the wilderness. Were there times of separation between God and Israel? Sure there were. God had sent the people into exile and captivity numerous times.

But make no mistake. This was redemptive separation. He called Israel into the wilderness so He could speak comfort to her. God never had a complete separation in mind. He is always faithful.

This is what He had called Hosea to live out before the children of Israel. His life was to display a love that could not be shaken. It was Christ's love being perfected in Hosea.

We all love the times in marriage that are 'for better'; but who are we to say He isn't good when He lets us enter into times that seem to be 'for worse'? Do we not believe that God has a plan? Do we stagger at His promises?

Certainly sexual unfaithfulness isn't the only problem prevalent in marriages today. But the answer is the same with any problem facing us in marriage. We must love as Christ loves. That isn't our natural tendency and it will be through trials and adversity that His love is placed in us. But in this He is good. He is God, and He is faithful.

10

The Israel of God

The Goodness of God in Racial Discrimination

The family of God is ethnically and culturally diverse. As Christians we not only permit such diversity, but we cherish it. This is because God Himself cherishes ethnic diversity. He is not color-blind; He is colorful. At His throne God welcomes worshipers 'from every nation, tribe, people and language' (Rev. 7:9). His plan of redemption is for the peoples of the world in all their rich variety.

Philip Graham Ryken

Hitler, the Klan and the Plan of God

When I think of all the horrors of racial discrimination, a few things come to mind. As an American, I think of the shameful evil of the American slave trade, which lasted from America's birth in 1776 until the Civil War era. So many people were treated horribly under the appalling conditions brought about by slavery. Basic human rights were stripped away as slaves were treated as animals to be bought and sold.

I think also of the Holocaust of World War II, and the insanity of Hitler. Nearly six million Jews lost their lives during the Holocaust, which was the result of Hitler's deep, vehement hatred for the Jewish people. This is interesting in that Hitler himself was probably partly Jewish, yet it speaks to the demonic origins of the man's hatred. Hitler had a plan of exterminating the Jews by whatever means necessary. Most died by being gassed, cooked alive or shot.

I've often thought, 'Where was the goodness of God then? Where was God's goodness at Auschwitz?' As Jews were being beaten and burned, raped and reviled, where was the goodness of God? As the slaves of the 1700-1800s were being treated as animals because of the color of their skin, where was God's goodness? And even today, as many still face different forms of racial discrimination, where is God and how does He show His goodness to those who are suffering?

I think part of man's depravity is that, because of pride, when a man looks at someone different than he, he automatically concludes that the differences are bad. Because man seems to see himself as the center of the universe, anything different from him is somehow 'less' —less good, less important, less impressive. We saw this tendency in Hitler. If you were handicapped, you were killed. If you had a flaw, you died. If you were unable to contribute to the creation of a master race, there was no reason for your existence, and you were killed.

But since when was being different bad? Since when was the white man better than the black man, or the German better than the Jew? Somehow we equate 'different' with 'inferior'. Let's take a minute to examine this idea.

Imagine it's a nice fall day. You and some friends decide it would be fun to take a drive through the mountains and look at all the trees and leaves. As you're driving you realize how beautiful all the leaves are, each the same color and shape and texture as the next; they're all identical! What beauty! Oh, wait.

That can't be right. We don't enjoy the uniformity of leaves in the fall. We enjoy the diversity. There's something wondrous about seeing the different colors as they blend together; the orange and red, brown and yellow. They look so stunning together.

I remember driving though the mountains of eastern Tennessee during the fall and thinking, 'God, what a wonderful Creator You are.' The different colors make fall such a beautiful season.

Sadly, if diversity of color creates beauty, many of our churches are looking pretty ugly these days. We have white churches and black churches, Asian churches and Hispanic churches. I wonder if heaven will be that way. Maybe the throne room will have different worship services, one service for the Asian, another for those of African descent. How about a Latin service? Don't forget the 'traditional service', for those of European origin. What do you think? I think not.

How is it that we're going to spend eternity worshiping together, yet we can't join as one for weekly worship?

'Well, Jamie, it's cultural. You understand, right?'

No, I don't. When I was saved, I became a citizen of a kingdom far beyond my German roots. I belong to something that transcends race. My allegiance isn't to the United States or to Germany. My home is in the kingdom of God. The moment I show anything less than Christ's love to those different than I, I bear witness to the fact that I'm not of that kingdom. In such a case, I am not His and He is not mine.

With that said, we are confident that God will triumph over the evil of racial segregation and will show Himself good in the midst of it.

The Israel of God

One of the clearest forms of racial prejudice in the Bible is found in the schism between the Jews and Greeks. If any race of people had a temptation toward racial pride, surely it would be the Jews. After all, they are God's chosen people. Yet Paul, a Jew himself, repeatedly denounces exclusivity of salvation as being only for the Jew. Take this passage in Colossians as an example.

> Do not lie to one another, since you have put off the old man with his deeds, and have put on the new man who is renewed in knowledge according to the image of Him who created him, where there is neither Greek nor Jew, circumcised nor uncircumcised, barbarian, Scythian, slave nor free, but Christ is all and in all. (Col. 3:9-11)

'Christ is all and in all' regardless of race or other divisions. The Jews of Paul's day wanted to point to their ritual of circumcision as a sign of superiority. Paul repeatedly attacked this legalistic tendency.

> In Him you were also circumcised with the circumcision made without hands, by putting off the body of the sins of the flesh, by the circumcision of Christ ... (Col. 2:11)

In the New Testament we see the unfolding of God's plan (although the firstfruits were seen in the Old Testament) and His goodness amidst the prejudice of Jewish exclusivism, in the revealing of what Paul called the 'Israel of God'.

> For in Christ Jesus neither circumcision nor uncircumcision avails anything, but a new creation. And as many as walk according to this rule, peace and mercy be upon them, and upon the Israel of God. (Gal. 6:15-16)

What is this 'Israel of God'? Paul better explains himself in his letter to the Romans.

> But it is not that the word of God has taken no effect. For they are not all Israel who are of Israel, nor are they all children because they are the seed of Abraham; but, 'In Isaac your

seed shall be called'. That is, those who are the children of the flesh, these are not the children of God; but the children of the promise are counted as the seed. (Rom. 9:6-8)

In other words, the true Israel of God (essentially another name for the church) is not comprised merely of those who are of the literal genealogy of Abraham, though I believe God does have a unique, future work of redemption for ethnic Israel, but are those who are 'children of promise', that is, both Jew and Gentile who are called out by grace into salvation.

And if you are Christ's, then you are Abraham's seed, and heirs according to the promise. (Gal. 3:29)

The requirement for being of Abraham's seed is of the Spirit and not the flesh. Faith in Christ is what links you to Abraham and to God's promise to him, not just Jewish ancestry. By grace, God grafts Gentiles into the promise of salvation, first given to Eve in Genesis 3:15, later given to Abraham, and sealed by the death and resurrection of Christ. Thus, as believers we are children of promise. This by no means implies that God has replaced the promise He made to the Jews with a promise to the Gentiles. Rather, Gentiles become partakers of the same promise; that promise remains for the Jew, but is expanded to include the Gentile.

And so we see God's goodness in that though this kingdom be riddled with the decadence of racial prejudice, there is a kingdom to come which will not be. This will be an everlasting kingdom to be seen and savored by all the nations of the earth.

Yes, all kings shall fall down before Him; all nations shall serve Him. (Ps. 72:11)

And men shall be blessed in Him; all nations shall call Him blessed. (Ps. 72:17b)

> Oh, let the nations be glad and sing for joy! For You shall judge the people righteously, and govern the nations on earth. (Ps. 67:4)

Every nation, race and people group has cause for joy. God's plan is that all people, yes, all races, will delight in Him alone, and that they will be His people, and He will govern them and be their God, regardless of race.

The Glory of God Among the Races

Finally, we know that in the culmination of time, the races of the earth will be seen and heard glorifying God around His throne.

> After these things I looked, and behold, a great multitude which no one could number, of all nations, tribes, peoples, and tongues, standing before the throne and before the Lamb, clothed with white robes, with palm branches in their hands, and crying out with a loud voice, saying, 'Salvation belongs to our God who sits on the throne, and to the Lamb!' (Rev. 7:9-10)

He is 'our God.' He doesn't belong to any one race, but is the Father to all who call upon His name. He pours out His spirit on '*all flesh*' (Acts 2:17). Have you called on His name? Has He wrought in you the work of salvation? If so, you get to take part in God's plan for the races, that each race honor and glorify His name forever. The great mockery of racism is the colorful kingdom of God.

11

Katrina: God's Messenger?

The Goodness of God in Natural Disasters

Lord, be pleased to shake my clay cottage before Thou throwest it down.

Thomas Fuller

God the Weatherman

I was ten years old in April of 1996. My family lived in a quiet neighborhood in Fort Smith, Arkansas. I'll never forget the night that put our small town on the national news. A large tornado ripped through the heart of our city, destroying countless homes and disturbing life in Fort Smith for months and years to come.

Thankfully, our home wasn't among those affected. But I vividly recall the grief of those around me whose lives were radically transformed by the storm. Many were left homeless, with no place to go.

I volunteered at a large Methodist church that had become a shelter for some of the thousands who had lost their homes. I remember working in the midst of the chaos, with people sprawled out everywhere with nothing left except the clothes on their back, and thinking, 'This is awful. What if I were in their shoes?' Natural disasters can have life-altering effects. The damage and suffering they cause are often catastrophic.

Think about the natural disasters that have affected the U.S.A. Almost every American who is old enough remembers Hurricane Katrina. On August 29, 2005, she blasted the shoreline of Louisiana and Mississippi in one of the most devastating natural disasters in American history. Katrina took the lives of 1,464 victims and destroyed an estimated 275,000 homes. The ruin left in the city of New Orleans and across the Gulf Coast is almost unmatched.

Outside the U.S.A., think about the massive earthquake and tsunami of 2011 that pillaged Japan and much of the Pacific regions, killing an estimated 18,000 or more people and leaving more than 400,000 people homeless. Or consider the horrendous earthquake that occurred in Haiti in 2010, killing around a quarter of a million people or more. What devastation!

Where is God when natural disasters occur? If He is Lord of all creation, why does He allow His creation to wreak such havoc? Some people believe that God put creation into motion, but now He just lets things take their natural course. In this view, He is kind of like a boy who puts a paper airplane to flight, letting natural laws control where it goes. However, the Bible portrays God as having a continual rule over creation. Indeed, God is Lord of all creation. He created all things by His Word, Christ (John 1:3), and He continues to uphold His creation by 'the word of His power' (Heb. 1:3). He continually sustains that which He created. Consider the words of Paul to the Colossians, speaking of Christ, Paul writes:

> He is the image of the invisible God, the firstborn over all creation. For by Him all things were created that are in heaven and that are on earth, visible and invisible, whether thrones or dominions or principalities or powers. All things were created through Him and for Him. And He is before all things, and in Him all things consist. (Col. 1:15-17)

Here we see a statement about both the past and the present. First, all things were created through Christ (past), and all things continue to consist and have their being through Him (present). Certainly, this statement encompasses more than the weather, but it must also include weather. Scripture records many accounts of natural disasters as coming by the hand of God. Let's examine some of these accounts and the purpose of God in them.

Redemptive Destruction

Since natural disasters have occurred throughout history, it is only expected that we see accounts of several throughout the Scriptures. The most obvious and devastating was the flood in the days of Noah (see Gen. 7). Genesis also recounts the destruction of Sodom and Gomorrah (Gen. 19:24). Ezekiel speaks of God's judgment on Israel as manifesting through natural disasters (Ezek. 13:13) and Jeremiah speaks of God judging Babylon in a like manner (Jer. 51:41-45). When we see the various disasters throughout Scripture, there is often a common theme: The Judgment of God. Why was there a flood in Noah's day? Because of the wickedness of man (Gen. 6:5). Why did God destroy Sodom and Gomorrah? Because of their perversion (Gen. 19). Why did Israel face judgment? Because of their foolish false prophets (Ezek. 13:1-3). Likewise, Babylon was destroyed because of her unrighteousness (Jer. 51).

The judgments of God are good. David speaks repeatedly in the Psalms of his personal love for the judgments of God. Consider Psalm 19:9-11.

> The fear of the Lord is clean, enduring forever;
> The judgments of the Lord are true and righteous altogether.
> More to be desired are they than gold,
> Yea, than much fine gold;
> Sweeter also than honey and the honeycomb.
> Moreover by them Your servant is warned,
> And in keeping them there is great reward. (Ps. 19:9-11)

David understood the value of the judgments of God. He understood that they were the means by which God kept him on the path leading to life. What else did David say?

> Who can understand his errors?
> Cleanse me from secret faults.
> Keep back Your servant from presumptuous sins;
> Let them not have dominion over me.
> Then I shall be blameless,
> And I shall be innocent of great transgression. (Ps. 19:12-13)

Often times, when we think of the judgment of God, we think of it in the context of eternal judgment. Certainly, in keeping with Scriptures such as Hebrew 6:2, we affirm the doctrine of eternal judgment as God's retributive punishment upon the wicked. However, that isn't the kind of judgment we're dealing with here. Here, David ascribes love for the judgments of God because they warn him and keep him in the way that is right. That is to say, in these judgments we see the redemptive heart of God, which fosters repentance in His people and shows the abundance of His grace.

We don't know the depths of evil in our own heart. There are faults within us buried so deeply that the grace of God has to reveal them. Yet, if God brings judgment on sin now – in the sense that He gives warning and brings to light the sin of a people – He can show His goodness by saving many from eternal judgment and fostering a spirit of repentance.

God did this time and time again with Israel. Consider the reference I sited earlier in Ezekiel 13:13. Indeed, God brings judgment on Israel in the form of 'stormy winds' and 'flooding rain' because of the words of their false prophets. This word of judgment continues into Ezekiel chapter 14. God highlights, through Ezekiel, the idolatry of Israel and gives further word concerning God's purpose in touching a land that has rebelled against Him. Yet in the end, God's word to Ezekiel concerning this judgment which God has put on Israel and her land is this:

> 'Yet behold, there shall be left in it a remnant who will be brought out, both sons and daughters; surely they will come out to you, and you will see their ways and their doings. Then you will be comforted concerning the disaster that I have brought upon Jerusalem, all that I have brought upon it. And they will comfort you, when you see their ways and their doings; and you shall know that I have done nothing without cause that I have done in it,' says the Lord GOD. (Ezek. 14:22-23)

In the end, God tells Ezekiel that the very disaster which brought calamity upon Israel will end up being a source of comfort. When Ezekiel sees the work of redemption that God brings about through the disaster, the Prophet's soul will rest. In other words, Ezekiel will see the destruction and its purpose, and thus call God good.

That God would foster redemption through natural disaster is in no way unique to Ezekiel. We see this same rhythm of disaster and redemption all throughout the text. In the days of the Prophet Joel, God sent judgment upon Israel in the form of locusts which devoured their land.

> Hear this, you elders, and give ear, all you inhabitants of the land! Has anything like this happened in your days, or even in the days of your fathers? Tell your children about it, let your children tell their children, and their children another generation. What the chewing locust left, the swarming locust has eaten; what the swarming locust left, the crawling locust has eaten; and what the crawling locust left, the consuming locust has eaten. Awake, you drunkards, and weep; and wail, all you drinkers of wine, because of the new wine, for it has been cut off from your mouth. (Joel 1:2-5)

With this judgment comes a call to repent and a word of promise after repentance has been granted. Watch how the same judgment-redemption 'rhythm' occurs in Joel.

First, God brings disaster on the land because of sin and unfaithfulness. Next, we see the redemptive heart of God, which in Joel is broken into two parts, (1) the call to repentance (2) the word of redemptive promise.

1. Call to repentance

> 'Now, therefore,' says the LORD, 'Turn to Me with all your heart, with fasting, with weeping, and with mourning.' So rend your heart, and not your garments; return to the LORD your God, for He is gracious and merciful, slow to anger, and of great kindness; and He relents from doing harm. Who knows if He will turn and relent, and leave a blessing behind Him – A grain offering and a drink offering for the LORD your God? (Joel 2:12-14)

2. Redemptive promise

> Then the LORD will be zealous for His land, and pity His people. The LORD will answer and say to His people, 'Behold,

> I will send you grain and new wine and oil, and you will be satisfied by them; I will no longer make you a reproach among the nations.' (Joel 2:18-19)

> 'So I will restore to you the years that the swarming locust has eaten, the crawling locust, the consuming locust, and the chewing locust, my great army which I sent among you. You shall eat in plenty and be satisfied, and praise the name of the LORD your God, who has dealt wondrously with you; And My people shall never be put to shame. Then you shall know that I am in the midst of Israel: I am the LORD your God and there is no other. My people shall never be put to shame.' (Joel 2:25-27)

Do you see it? Did God send the destruction? Yes, but the destruction was meant to foster repentance in the people of God. After true repentance is fostered in the heart of the people, God promises redemption and restoration. For the people of God, such God-ordained affliction and destruction is always meant for our good. God, being a good Father, disciplines and chastises His children, through natural disaster or other means, that He may draw us into closer fellowship. He is good!

Does God destroy? Yes. Are there times when destruction is not redemptive, in the sense that it does not foster repentance or life? Sure, again see Jeremiah 51, God's judgment on Babylon, who were a people not called by God's name. We've seen God's goodness in the death of the wicked earlier in the chapter on death. However, we see over and over in Scripture this purpose and plan of God to use destruction, even over cities, land, and geography to produce life in those who are His own, foster repentance, and show forth His work of redemption. Therefore, in natural disasters we say God is good.

The Groans of Creation
The Bible also refers to natural disasters in another light as well. Jesus spoke of natural disasters that would precede His second

coming (Matt. 24:7). Paul also spoke of the earth undergoing labor pangs, awaiting its redemption at the end of the age.

> For the creation was subjected to futility, not willingly, but because of Him who subjected it in hope; because the creation itself also will be delivered from the bondage of corruption into the glorious liberty of the children of God. For we know that the whole creation groans and labors with birth pangs together until now. (Rom. 8:20-22)

The earth itself is tired of the corruption and sin of man. The earth didn't want to be part of man's futility, but was subjected to it in hope. What hope? The hope of redemption. The earth groans for redemption! We see an earthquake or a tornado, a tsunami or a hurricane, and suddenly we realize that the earth is telling us something. Contrary to what post-modernists may say, it isn't merely telling us of pollution or global warming; it's telling us of sin and judgment. It's telling us of the soon-coming return of Christ.

If we sit in our piousness and false forms of religion, claiming 'peace, peace,' when the whole time there is no peace and everyone is being ravaged by sin, isn't it the kindness of God to send a tsunami to wake us up? Isn't it His kindness to send us a reminder of a coming King of glory, who will sit and judge the world of sin?

Indeed, God is good even in times of natural disaster. He takes the tsunami and brings forth salvation. He takes the raging storm to foster redemption. God is good! He is mighty to save!

12

Hope for Every Trial

The Goodness of God in His Purpose and Plan for Suffering

They gave our Master a crown of thorns. Why do we hope for a crown of roses?

Martin Luther

When I set out to write this book, I felt impressed by the Lord to take a very practical approach and address common sources of suffering that most people encounter. As Christians, we have to know how to cope with affliction from a biblical viewpoint. We've looked at many examples of how God's goodness may be found in the midst of common forms of suffering such as sickness, death, poverty and rejection, but there are so many other forms of suffering, it's impossible to address them all. Nonetheless, the biblical and theological truths remain constant no matter what form the suffering itself may take. The purpose of this chapter is to examine the basic biblical truths to be found in all forms of suffering, and to demonstrate how God uses them to show His goodness. No matter what my pain looks like, these things are certain.

Suffering Unites Us With Christ

> Beloved, do not think it strange concerning the fiery trial which is to try you, as though some strange thing happened to you; but rejoice to the extent that you partake of Christ's sufferings, that when His glory is revealed, you may also be glad with exceeding joy. If you are reproached for the name of Christ, blessed are you, for the Spirit of glory and of God rests upon you. On their part He is blasphemed, but on your part He is glorified. (1 Pet. 4:12-14)

Look again at the words of Peter. *'But rejoice to the extent that you partake of Christ's sufferings, that when His glory is revealed, you may also be glad with exceeding joy'* (v. 13). On the day when His glory is revealed, not everyone will have joy. There will be those who, because of their unrepentant heart, cry for rocks to fall on them at the return of Christ in His glory. But for those who have partnered with Christ in His sufferings, it will be a most glorious day.

There is much to be said concerning the ways in which suffering unites us with Christ. Jesus is revealed to us in the Old Testament as the suffering Servant (Isa. 53). The very identity and function of Christ during His earthly ministry were tied to suffering. He was as a Lamb led to the slaughter (Isa. 53:7). He learned obedience by the things He suffered (Heb. 5:8). If we are to be conformed to His likeness and take on His image, suffering becomes inescapable. As Paul says ...

> The Spirit Himself bears witness with our spirit that we are
> children of God, and if children, then heirs—heirs of God and
> joint heirs with Christ, if indeed we suffer with Him, that we
> may also be glorified together. For I consider that the sufferings
> of this present time are not worthy to be compared with the
> glory which shall be revealed in us. (Rom. 8:16-18)

How can we compare any type of suffering with the glory that
is ours in Christ? We can't! I pray that we would understand the
magnitude of Christ's glory. It's far beyond any comparison. His
glory is the perfection of beauty, the one thing that is able to
truly satisfy our hearts eternally. This glory awaits those who
suffer with Christ. This is the good news of the gospel.

Anything I must endure in this life is but a light, momentary
affliction compared with the abundance of Christ's glory, of
which I will partake in the age to come. When I understand
that the temporal sufferings of this age only prepare me for the
unmatched inheritance of Christ, I, like James, can count my
sufferings as pure joy (James 1:2). After all, my trials are uniting
me with Christ.

Therefore I will be content no matter what state I'm in,
knowing that God is working to draw me closer to Himself,
even in affliction and suffering.

Suffering Brings Honor to God

The high aim of Christianity is the glorification of God forever.
The true Christian is always seeking to glorify God by every
means possible. In light of this, let's review the text as found in
First Peter.

> If you are reproached for the name of Christ, blessed are you,
> for the Spirit of glory and of God rests upon you. On their part
> He is blasphemed, but on your part He is glorified. (1 Pet. 4:14)

What a paradox! By my sufferings Christ is glorified. Let this be the litmus test for the believer: that we would take joy in suffering so that Christ would be glorified through it. This is not suffering so that we gain anything (although we do gain through suffering), but so that He may gain the glory due His name.

We must love the glorification of Christ more than our own comfort. True love puts itself on the line; it promotes the object of its affection above self. If I really love Christ, my greatest desire is to see Him glorified no matter the cost. If my suffering brings Christ glory, then bring on the suffering!Why are we so passionate about the glorification of Christ? Because He has shown us, through grace, the depths of His worthiness. When I look at the splendor of what Christ accomplished on the cross and all that He has done for me, the hopeless sinner, I am filled with a passion to see the Lamb who was slain for me receive all the glory and praise that is rightfully His. A true revelation of Christ's love demands of me that the response of my heart be that this wonderful King be lauded, praised, magnified and glorified as He should be, even in my sufferings.

Suffering Unites Us With the Cross

Paul's letter to the church at Galatia differs from most of his other epistles. It's common for Paul, when writing to a church, to first commend the people for the things they're doing well, and then address any concerns he has for them. However, in Galatians Paul never gives way for compliments, but spends the entire book addressing areas of weakness. It becomes evident that those in Galatia were stuck in the religious duties of Judaism, unable to enjoy the freedoms of grace in Christ. For this reason Paul writes:

> As many as desire to make a good showing in the flesh, these would compel you to be circumcised, only that they may not

suffer persecution for the cross of Christ. For not even those who are circumcised keep the law, but they desire to have you circumcised that they may boast in your flesh. But God forbid that I should boast except in the cross of our Lord Jesus Christ, by whom the world has been crucified to me, and I to the world. (Gal. 6:12-14)

Teaching the cross offends many. Teaching that salvation comes by grace alone is guaranteed to offend many. Man wants to equate salvation with some good work he has done. In Paul's day the issue was circumcision, among other things. Some teachers said, 'Obey the law. Be circumcised, and you'll be saved.' In our day the issue is praying the right prayer, or consenting to certain theological truths. We say, 'If you want to be saved, pray this prayer, believe our doctrinal statement, give to our offerings and, brother, you're saved.' But the problem we face now is the same problem Paul had then. Salvation can only come by grace, not works. Whether you're circumcised or not isn't the issue. Instead, it comes down to a simple question: Was God's grace given to you for new life?

I agree with Paul. Salvation is only by grace and not because of anything I have done, or could have done. It's simply by God's grace! This is what Martin Luther and so many others fought for. They were passionate in their desire that we would see salvation as truly coming from grace alone. This is the message of the cross. Paul preached it, and was ridiculed. The founders of the Protestant Reformation preached it, and were killed. If you dare stand on grace alone, you too will be hated by many. But we have a promise.

For if we have been united together in the likeness of His death, certainly we also shall be in the likeness of His resurrection … (Rom. 6:5)

THOUGH HE SLAY ME

If I embrace the cross and its message of salvation by grace alone, I will also join in His resurrection. Just as He came from death to life, I also will be taken from spiritual death into spiritual life. Take comfort from these words. Though others may scoff at you now, you shall reign with Christ. You have an inheritance that is more wonderful, more precious, than words could ever describe (Eph. 1:11-12).

Although it is freely given, we must understand that this grace is not a cheap grace. It has a price tag that was more than you or I would ever want to pay. Yet Christ paid the price. We can now enjoy the fruits of this wonderful grace only because of the blood Christ shed on the cross. The cross was so necessary. Though it was messy, bloody and horrifically painful, it was abundantly necessary. There was no way for any of us to enter into true life without there first being a death. Christ had to die, atoning for sin, so that we may live. Salvation always necessitates death. While Christ fulfilled this on the cross, it remains that we also must die to ourselves if we are to live in Christ. As Christ Himself said ...

> Whoever desires to come after Me, let him deny himself, and take up his cross, and follow Me. (Mark 8:34b)

We too must die. Not in atonement for sin—Christ did that—but in obedience to Christ.

> For if we have been united together in the likeness of His death, certainly we also shall be in the likeness of His resurrection, knowing this, that our old man was crucified with Him, that the body of sin might be done away with, that we should no longer be slaves of sin. For he who has died has been freed from sin. Now if we died with Christ, we believe that we shall also live with Him ... (Rom. 6:5-8)

146

Because of this we say, 'Thank God for sufferings, which unite us to the cross and lead us to salvation.'

God Uses Suffering to Foster Salvation

We have clearly established that salvation is available only through grace. Yet it's important to understand that God can use different means to bring that about. I think the Bible lays clear groundwork to show that He sometimes uses suffering to bring about salvation. Again, the clearest example of this is the cross itself. The things Christ suffered made the way for salvation.

But let's also consider Saul. He was struck blind while on the road to Damascus, and this was the process God used to convert Saul the persecutor and transform him into Paul the apostle. As an apostle of Christ, Paul wrote to the Corinthian church, encouraging them, telling them that his suffering was for their consolation and salvation.

> Blessed be the God and Father of our Lord Jesus Christ, the Father of mercies and God of all comfort,who comforts us in all our tribulation, that we may be able to comfort those who are in any trouble, with the comfort with which we ourselves are comforted by God. For as the sufferings of Christ abound in us, so our consolation also abounds through Christ. Now if we are afflicted, it is for your consolation and salvation, which is effective for enduring the same sufferings which we also suffer. Or if we are comforted, it is for your consolation and salvation. (2 Cor. 1:3-6)

Finally, consider the Jews. For centuries they have endured suffering because they are God's chosen people; yet we know the day is coming when Israel will be saved, and the purpose of their suffering will be realized (Zech. 12:10).

When we looked at the goodness of God even in the midst of natural disasters we saw how God, in His goodness, could bring about calamity in order to foster salvation. This is true of all suffering; God uses our trials to draw us to Himself.

God Uses Suffering to Foster Sanctification

But what does sanctification have to do with suffering? According to the life of Jesus, everything! Hebrews chapter five helps point this out.

> So also Christ did not glorify Himself to become High Priest, but it was He who said to Him:
> 'You are My Son,
> Today I have begotten You.'
> As He also says in another place:
> 'You are a priest forever
> According to the order of Melchizedek';
> who, in the days of His flesh, when He had offered up prayers and supplications, with vehement cries and tears to Him who was able to save Him from death, and was heard because of His godly fear, though He was a Son, yet He learned obedience by the things which He suffered. (Heb. 5:5-8)

Jesus learned obedience by the things He suffered. We see here a direct correlation between the sufferings of Christ and His learning of obedience. Why would the Son of God need to learn obedience? Isn't He already perfectly obedient? Yes, He is. But the sufferings of Christ taught Him what it was like to be human, so that He could sympathize with our weaknesses. The writer of Hebrews unfolds for us Christ's role as our great High Priest.

> For we do not have a High Priest who cannot sympathize with our weaknesses, but was in all points tempted as we are, yet without sin. (Heb. 4:15)

Christ became our sympathetic High Priest by enduring temptation. Strapping on humanity was a form of suffering for Christ. Just imagine what it must have been like to trade complete divinity for humanity (though Christ always retained His divinity). By becoming human and enduring and overcoming temptation and suffering, Christ became our great, sympathetic High Priest. He knows of our sufferings and can be truly sympathetic in them because He also once suffered.

Have you ever had someone come to you during a time of grief and say, 'Oh, I know how you feel.' As you wipe away the tears, you think, 'No, you don't. You have no clue how I feel.' They're trying to be sympathetic, but if they've never experienced what you're experiencing, then they cannot truly relate to how you feel. It's as though I were to go to my wife while she is in the middle of labor, giving birth to a baby, and say, 'Honey, I know how you feel!' What? I have absolutely no way to truly sympathize with that. If I say I do, my efforts to comfort her are vain.

Jesus, the great High Priest, does not offer vain, thoughtless words of comfort. He is able to serve as the great High Priest precisely because He learned through suffering.

If the Son of God needed to learn obedience through suffering, what does that say for you and me? I've seen in my own life that it has been my sufferings that have drawn me closer to Christ. Haven't you?

Consider Jacob. In Genesis we read:

> Then Jacob was left alone; and a Man wrestled with him until the breaking of day. Now when He saw that He did not prevail against him, He touched the socket of his hip; and the socket of Jacob's hip was out of joint as He wrestled with him. And He said, 'Let Me go, for the day breaks.' But he said, 'I will not let You go unless You bless me!' So He said to him, 'What is your name?' He said, 'Jacob.'

> And He said, 'Your name shall no longer be called Jacob, but Israel; for you have struggled with God and with men, and have prevailed.' (Gen. 32:24-28)

Jacob's sanctification came as he wrestled with God. The outcome of this night of struggle was that Jacob emerged with a new name, which is symbolic of conversion in the Old Testament. After wrestling with God, Jacob's hip socket was out of joint. Jacob—Israel—would always walk with a limp thereafter to remind him of the time that he saw God face to face, and of his dependency on Him.

Even so, the love of God may cause you some trouble; it may cause you to limp just so you will know who you are without Him. I know I've had struggles, and my walk in Christ is with a limp. But that's all right. My limp reminds me of my dependence on God, and of my need for a Savior.

Suffering Identifies Us as Sons of God

> ... so that we ourselves boast of you among the churches of God for your patience and faith in all your persecutions and tribulations that you endure, which is manifest evidence of the righteous judgment of God, that you may be counted worthy of the kingdom of God, for which you also suffer ... (2 Thess. 1:4-5)

> Remember the word that I [Jesus] said to you, 'A servant is not greater than his master.' If they persecuted Me, they will also persecute you. (John 15:20a)

The world hated Jesus because He bore the fruit of righteousness, and men preferred their darkness to the light (John 3:19). Sadly, the world hasn't changed; men still hate righteousness and love depravity. Therefore, if you bear the fruit of righteousness you will be hated. However, in this we can rejoice in that we are being like Christ—both in bearing good fruit and in being hated for it. And we know that we are His if we bear the fruit of righteousness. This isn't the fruit of mere religion, nor is it the cloying fruit of being a 'good person'. No, I am speaking of the fruit of true righteousness that comes from Christ Himself. And though we be hated for it by the world, our consolation lies in the fact that we are His forever!

There is truly joy in persecution. Recall again the words of Paul to those of Thessalonica:

> ... we ourselves boast of you among the churches of God for your patience and faith in all your persecutions and tribulations that you endure, which is manifest evidence of the righteous judgment of God, that you may be counted worthy of the kingdom of God, for which you also suffer ... (2 Thess. 1:4-5)

Paul cited their persecution and tribulation as evidence that the Thessalonians were children of God. '*You will know them by their fruits*' (Matt. 7:16). May it be said of us that we bear the name of Christ in the fruit of our suffering.

Paul also elsewhere spoke of His own partnering with Christ's suffering.

> I now rejoice in my sufferings for you, and fill up in my flesh what is lacking in the afflictions of Christ, for the sake of His body, which is the church ... (Col. 1:24)

Paul is certainly not implying that Christ's sufferings lacked anything by way of atoning for sin. Rather, he is merely addressing the fact that he takes joy in taking up the mantle of suffering which Christ left and being the present-day witness of Christ's suffering by demonstration to those in Colossae. John Piper wonderfully explains it.

> What's missing is the in-person presentation of Christ's sufferings to the people for whom He died. The afflictions are

lacking in the sense that they are not seen and known among the nations. They must be carried by ministers of the gospel. And those ministers of the gospel fill up what is lacking in the afflictions of Christ by extending them to others. [1]

Our present sufferings allow us to show God's goodness to others as they see our suffering. We take up our cross in honor of His name. Speaking of Paul, Matthew Henry writes:

He had a certain rate and measure of suffering for Christ assigned him; and, as his sufferings were agreeable to that appointment, so he was still filling up more and more what was behind, or remained of them to his share. [2]

If Christ suffered and was persecuted, we also as His children will suffer and be persecuted. However, this assignment of grace gives us hope; that just as He died and was raised again, so we also, after the suffering appointed for us, will be raised to newness of life.

Suffering Causes Us to Know God's Comfort

Blessed be the God and Father of our Lord Jesus Christ, the Father of mercies and God of all comfort, who comforts us in all our tribulation, that we may be able to comfort those who are in any trouble, with the comfort with which we ourselves are comforted by God. For as the sufferings of Christ abound in us, so our consolation also abounds through Christ. (2 Cor. 1:3-5)

If we're never in need of comfort and consolation, how will we know God's amazing comfort? My sufferings put me in a place where I have to lean on the comfort of Christ.

---

1. John Piper, 'Filling Up What Is Lacking in Christ's Afflictions', Desiring God: http://www.desiringgod.org/resource-library/conference-messages/filling-up-what-is-lacking-in-christs-afflictions#/listen/full (March 10, 2011).

2. Matthew Henry, *Matthew Henry's Commentary* (Peabody, MA; Hendrickson Publishers, 1991), p. 608.

Yea, though I walk through the valley of the shadow of death,
I will fear no evil;
For You are with me;
Your rod and Your staff, they comfort me. (Ps. 23:4)

How did David know the comfort of God? He had to walk through the valley of the shadow of death. We've seen that God could have maintained a sinless utopia, free of sin. But what if Adam and Eve had never fallen? We wouldn't know the wonders and beauty of the cross. God could have arranged life so that there were no times of suffering; but then what would our testimony of God's comfort be? Suffering comes, but in it we learn of God's wonderful comfort.

Imagine the comfort that Paul and Silas must have felt as they sat in prison. They were there because Christ's power through them had freed a slave girl of a demonic spirit—depriving her masters of the income she was generating for them. When they found out that Paul and Silas had ruined their money-making scheme, they had the men of God arrested. And what was their response?

But at midnight Paul and Silas were praying and singing hymns to God ... (Acts 16:25a)

If you were in prison, what would make you want to pray and sing hymns? I've been in prisons—I've done a lot of prison ministry. They are not joyful places. Yet even in that prison, Paul and Silas found deep comfort in the midst of their persecution and affliction. That had to have honored Christ.

I wonder how much we honor the Lord when we, in our sufferings, go deep to the source of our joy and rely on the comforts found in Christ? We can't despise our outward sufferings. We must rest in the comfort that is found in Christ. This honors and pleases the Lord.

Suffering Creates an Earnest Expectation of Things to Come

> For I consider that the sufferings of this present time are not worthy to be compared with the glory which shall be revealed in us. (Rom. 8:18)

Paul didn't complain about his sufferings because he knew how small they were in comparison with what he would gain in Christ. We first saw this principle when we looked at God's goodness in sickness, but it deserves to be repeated. Suffering shows me the futility of this world and how temporal this age is, and puts longings within me for the eternal age to come. It reminds me that my citizenship isn't in the kingdoms of men, but in a coming kingdom.

As we look toward this future revelation of glory, we are filled with unspeakable joy and anticipation as we await the coming of our Bridegroom, Jesus. We are to be like the five wise virgins of Matthew 25 who were found ready, waiting and eagerly watching for the coming of their bridegroom.

Paul makes very clear what we're expectantly waiting for.

> For we know that the whole creation groans and labors with birth pangs together until now. Not only that, but we also who have the firstfruits of the Spirit, even we ourselves groan within ourselves, eagerly waiting for the adoption, the redemption of our body. (Rom. 8:22-23)

We await the consummation of our salvation in Christ Jesus. We will be fully His. He will be fully ours, and we will receive in full the Spirit of adoption, being rightful children of God the Father, while also the adorned bride of Christ.

Our physical body will be redeemed from mortality with all its pain, and we will be given new bodies, which are immortal and fully capable of enjoying the beauties and pleasures of Christ forever.

These are the things that make suffering seem so insignificant in comparison. Because of this, we gladly embrace our cross, with its implications of death and suffering, knowing that the resurrection is to a life so glorious that no hedonistic climax in this life could ever compare. Suffering serves as a constant reminder that for the believer, the best is yet to come.

Suffering Can Renew the Mind

> Finally, brethren, whatever things are true, whatever things are noble, whatever things are just, whatever things are pure, whatever things are lovely, whatever things are of good report, if there is any virtue and if there is anything praiseworthy— meditate on these things. (Phil. 4:8)

> If then you were raised with Christ, seek those things which are above, where Christ is, sitting at the right hand of God.Set your mind on things above, not on things on the earth.For you died, and your life is hidden with Christ in God. (Col. 3:1-3)

The carnal mind is enmity toward God (see Romans 8:7), but the renewed mind can be a wonderful tool when purified by God in sanctification. Suffering can serve as the great sanctifier, which renews our mind. It's easy to let our minds become lost in vain imaginings or thoughts, but when suffering comes, we begin to reevaluate what we hold to be important. Suddenly, the frivolous things we used to daydream about for hours don't even enter our minds.

When our son, Judah, was born with so many complications, the things I had been thinking about in the days before his birth suddenly didn't matter. It was time to set my mind on things above. It was time to constantly remind myself of the things of

God, to have thoughts that built up my faith. Otherwise, the fears would have overcome me. All the doubts and 'what if's' could have played with me to make me question what I knew about the goodness of God. This is why it's so important to keep your mind on godly things. Our daily thoughts should remain on the wonderful things of God.

> Blessed is the man
> Who walks not in the counsel of the ungodly,
> Nor stands in the path of sinners,
> Nor sits in the seat of the scornful;
> But his delight is in the law of the Lord,
> And in His law he meditates day and night. (Ps. 1:1-2)

We must meditate on Him day and night. I wish it didn't take tragedy and suffering to focus our minds on Christ. But if it does, thank God for that suffering which helps us to renew our minds in the excellencies of Christ.

Suffering Fosters Love

Consider this biblical example.

> Then one of the Pharisees asked Him to eat with him. And He went to the Pharisee's house, and sat down to eat. And behold, a woman in the city who was a sinner, when she knew that Jesus sat at the table in the Pharisee's house, brought an alabaster flask of fragrant oil, and stood at His feet behind Him weeping; and she began to wash His feet with her tears, and wiped them with the hair of her head; and she kissed His feet and anointed them with the fragrant oil. Now when the Pharisee who had invited Him saw this, he spoke to himself, saying, 'This Man, if He were a prophet, would know who and what manner of woman this is who is touching Him, for she is a sinner.'
>
> And Jesus answered and said to him, 'Simon, I have something to say to you.'

So he said, 'Teacher, say it.'

'There was a certain creditor who had two debtors. One owed five hundred denarii, and the other fifty. And when they had nothing with which to repay, he freely forgave them both. Tell Me, therefore, which of them will love him more?'

Simon answered and said, 'I suppose the one whom he forgave more.'

And He said to him, 'You have rightly judged.' Then He turned to the woman and said to Simon, 'Do you see this woman? I entered your house; you gave Me no water for My feet, but she has washed My feet with her tears and wiped them with the hair of her head. You gave Me no kiss, but this woman has not ceased to kiss My feet since the time I came in. You did not anoint My head with oil, but this woman has anointed My feet with fragrant oil. Therefore I say to you, her sins, which are many, are forgiven, for she loved much. But to whom little is forgiven, the same loves little.' (Luke 7:36-47)

This woman had lived a very hard life. She had lived in sin that brought on suffering and pain. Yet God used all she had been through to develop a love that was deeper than anyone had imagined. She loved Christ because of the goodness of God in her sufferings. Religion rejected her. Christ embraced her, and took her broken pieces and made her whole. Suffering definitely has a unique way of fostering love.

Consider this hypothetical example. There was a man named Joe who lived in the Depression era. Joe never had much and was very poor for most of his life. Around the age of eighteen, he met an attractive young girl named Sarah. Sarah hadn't ever had much either, but the two fell in love, got married, and started a family. Joe, a factory employee, worked hard to provide for his family. After several years of marriage, Joe and Sarah decided to start their own business. They had a rough start and, after the first year, wondered if they had made the right decision. After all, Joe had been making more money as a factory worker. But as they discussed the matter, they decided together to keep the business and make it work. The next several years were slow, but they made steady progress. Over time, their business became very successful. The years of struggle and strife had finally paid off! Imagine the joy that couple must have felt. They had walked hand in hand through difficult times, but finally all their sacrifices paid off. They enjoyed many years of success, the result of their steadfastness in difficult times. Because of all they had gone through to get to a place of success, they remained grounded and humble. Their years of suffering and struggle, which required them to bind closer together, fostered in both of them deep-rooted love and commitment for one another.

This is a profound truth. The sufferings my wife and I have endured with Judah have drawn us together in ways nothing else could have. We have had to learn to depend on each other in the most difficult of times. God has called us to the unique challenge of caring for our special-needs child, which for us has involved many sleepless, tear-filled nights, trying to care for Judah, while being unsure of what he needed. While we have many family members and friends who love us dearly and want to help when they can, these agonizing nights alone at home, have been the times God has used to draw us closer together.

God has ordained suffering for many redemptive purposes. All of His ways are good! For every trial, there's hope. Behind every test, there is a testimony. Allow God to move in your life and use suffering to unfold His perfect plan in you.

13

Behold, it is Finished

The Goodness of God in His Eventual Triumph Over Suffering

Afflictions are light when compared with what we really deserve. They are light when compared with the sufferings of the Lord Jesus. But perhaps their real lightness is best seen by comparing them with the weight of glory which is awaiting us.

A.W. Pink

The Final End

We've seen many answers to the question of how a good God could allow suffering, but there remains the one ultimate answer. Ultimately, He won't. God will, at His appointed time, put an end to all suffering and evil. True biblical eschatology (the study of end times) leads us to an understanding of God's goodness, both in the suffering and tribulation of the last days, and in His final obliteration of that suffering.

The failure of modern American eschatology over the past 100 years is that it has given many believers an escapist mentality.

We've been taught that Christians won't have to suffer at the end of the age; but Jesus gave a different depiction of the last days. Let's recall the teachings of Christ on this subject.

> Now as He sat on the Mount of Olives, the disciples came to Him privately, saying, 'Tell us, when will these things be? And what will be the sign of Your coming, and of the end of the age?'

> And Jesus answered and said to them: 'Take heed that no one deceives you. For many will come in My name, saying, "I am the Christ," and will deceive many. And you will hear of wars and rumors of wars. See that you are not troubled; for all these things must come to pass, but the end is not yet. For nation will rise against nation, and kingdom against kingdom. And there will be famines, pestilences, and earthquakes in various places. All these are the beginning of sorrows.

> Then they will deliver you up to tribulation and kill you, and you will be hated by all nations for My name's sake. And then many will be offended, will betray one another, and will hate one another. Then many false prophets will rise up and deceive many. And because lawlessness will abound, the love of many will grow cold. But he who endures to the end shall be saved. And this gospel of the kingdom will be preached in all the world as a witness to all the nations, and then the end will come.' (Matt. 24:3-14)

Jesus didn't give His disciples a hope of escaping tribulation. In fact, He promised them tribulation. Yet we know that He always had the Father's goodness in focus. So how can this coming tribulation serve the goodness of God?

As always, the wisdom behind such a seeming contradiction is more than we can naturally understand. But as we let Scripture interpret Scripture we begin to see the beauty of how God has ordained the end to come. Consider the following.

The Value of Final Tribulation for the Jew

Jeremiah also knew there was a coming tribulation at the end of the age. Read his words concerning Christ's second coming.

> Alas! For that day is great,
>
> So that none is like it;
>
> And it is the time of Jacob's trouble,
>
> But he shall be saved out of it. (Jer. 30:7)

Jeremiah illuminated the primary purpose behind the tribulation. He calls this time '*the time of Jacob's trouble*', which refers to God's dealing with the nation of Israel. God has promised Israel salvation as His chosen people. Though He cut them off for a season in order to have mercy on the Gentiles, He will be faithful to the promise He made. Jeremiah makes this clear when he says, '*but he* [Israel] *shall be saved out of it*'. It will be this trouble, this tribulation, which brings Israel into salvation. There are those who contend that the phrase, '*he shall be saved out of it*', means that Israel will not face tribulation at all. In that case, why would it be called 'Jacob's Trouble'? The grammar clearly suggests that the trouble belongs to Jacob (Israel). But they will be saved out of it in the manner Christ set forth when He said, '*unless those days were shortened, no flesh would be saved; but for the elect's sake those days will be shortened*' (Matt. 24:22). The days do come, tribulation does come; yet for the sake of the elect (Israel and the saved Gentiles) those days will be shortened and brought to a timely halt. Thus we are saved out of it.

The Value of Tribulation in the End and the Ultimate Age of Grace

It will be a wondrous day when Christ comes to receive His church, not only for the Jews, but also for Gentiles who have been saved by grace. At the end of the tribulation, after God has purified His people, He will return to earth to gather together those who are His, and with Him we shall always be! This is what really puts the 'good' into the 'Good News'. When Christ comes, He comes with a two-fold agenda. First, He will come to gather His elect, and secondly, He will come to judge the world of sin. Jesus' teaching confirmed this (Matt. 25:31-46).

Christ will come as Savior for the redeemed, but for the unredeemed He comes as Judge. He divides the nations, the righteous from the unrighteous. John foresaw this coming judgment while he was exiled on Patmos.

> Then I looked, and behold, a white cloud, and on the cloud sat One like the Son of Man, having on His head a golden crown, and in His hand a sharp sickle. And another angel came out of the temple, crying with a loud voice to Him who sat on the cloud, 'Thrust in Your sickle and reap, for the time has come for You to reap, for the harvest of the earth is ripe.' So He who sat on the cloud thrust in His sickle on the earth, and the earth was reaped.
>
> Then another angel came out of the temple which is in heaven, he also having a sharp sickle.
>
> And another angel came out from the altar, who had power over fire, and he cried with a loud cry to him who had the sharp sickle, saying, 'Thrust in your sharp sickle and gather the clusters of the vine of the earth, for her grapes are fully ripe.' So the angel thrust his sickle into the earth and gathered the vine of the earth, and threw it into the great winepress of the wrath of God. And the winepress was trampled outside the city, and blood came out of the winepress, up to the horses' bridles, for one thousand six hundred furlongs. (Rev. 14:14-20)

Christ is the great Judge. The magnitude of His judgment reflects the magnitude of His hatred toward sin. The degree to which

God is holy is the degree to which He judges sin. This passage shows the lengths to which Christ goes in order to judge man's sin. This is His vengeance. He has said, 'It is mine to avenge; I will repay' (see Deut. 32:35). So He shall avenge and repay the Beast (Antichrist), the false prophet and all who deny Him the glory due His name.

After the gathering together of believers and the judgment of sinners, the Lord will bind Satan for 1,000 years, and we who are believers will reign on earth with Christ for that 1,000 years (Rev. 20). At the end of 1,000 years Satan will be released for a short time for a final ultimatum. Satan will go out to deceive the nations, but will be met with the judgment of God. This is no temporary judgment; this is the final, everlasting judgment of God on Satan, sin and suffering.

> Now when the thousand years have expired, Satan will be released from his prison and will go out to deceive the nations which are in the four corners of the earth, Gog and Magog, to gather them together to battle, whose number is as the sand of the sea. They went up on the breadth of the earth and surrounded the camp of the saints and the beloved city. And fire came down from God out of heaven and devoured them. The devil, who deceived them, was cast into the lake of fire and brimstone where the beast and the false prophet are. And they will be tormented day and night forever and ever.

> Then I saw a great white throne and Him who sat on it, from whose face the earth and the heaven fled away. And there was found no place for them. And I saw the dead, small and great, standing before God, and books were opened. And another book was opened, which is the Book of Life. And the dead were judged according to their works, by the things which were written in the books. The sea gave up the dead who were in it, and Death and Hades delivered up the dead who were in

them. And they were judged, each one according to his works. Then Death and Hades were cast into the lake of fire. This is the second death. And anyone not found written in the Book of Life was cast into the lake of fire.(Rev. 20:7-15)

God never starts anything He can't finish. It would be absurd for a God of love to allow man to fall into sin and live in the sewage of depravity that sin brings—unless He was able to see the end from the beginning. And He does! When God allowed sin to enter in, it was for the purpose of showing us God's great glory and His power over sin. It may seem unfair to subject humanity to suffering in order for God to display the glory of His name, unless you see that it is by that very suffering that we are able to aptly cherish the goodness of God in delivering and sustaining us in the suffering that we rightfully deserved. The flawed wisdom of man will reject these truths. But they remain needful in our understanding of what God ordained within suffering.

The Ultimatum in the Goodness of God in Suffering

What we see in Revelation chapter 20 is the consummation of Christ's triumph over sin and suffering forever. Therefore, it remains that the goodness of God in suffering ends with His complete victory over it. When we understand these future events, we're able to see Christ as the conquering Victor that He is, and thus delight in Him all the more.

Once Christ defeats Satan and suffering, He will establish a new heaven and earth, and there we will enjoy all His delights forever.

Now I saw a new heaven and a new earth, for the first heaven and the first earth had passed away. Also there was no more sea. Then I, John, saw the holy city, New Jerusalem, coming down out of heaven from God, prepared as a bride adorned for her husband. And I heard a loud voice from heaven saying,

'Behold, the tabernacle of God is with men, and He will dwell with them, and they shall be His people. God Himself will be with them and be their God. And God will wipe away every tear from their eyes; there shall be no more death, nor sorrow, nor crying. There shall be no more pain, for the former things have passed away.' Then He who sat on the throne said, 'Behold, I make all things new.' And He said to me, 'Write, for these words are true and faithful.' (Rev. 21:1-5)

That city is my home. My citizenship is not of earth, nor of any kingdom of earth. Instead, it is of this coming city, the New Jerusalem, whose Builder and Maker is God (Heb. 11:10).

Knowing that such a city awaits me, I gladly endure the suffering of this age. I proudly wear the name 'pilgrim' in this life, because of what's to come in the next. Paul had the same thing in mind, the same city in view, when he wrote:

For I consider that the sufferings of this present time are not worthy to be compared with the glory which shall be revealed in us. (Rom. 8:18)

Does suffering exist? Yes, it does. Does God ordain it with His own set purposes? Yes, and His purposes are wonderful. But will He eventually put an end to suffering, once and for all? Yes! Yes, He will. He will show Himself victorious and mighty, and we shall forever reign with Him, beholding the beauties of His holiness.

Praise God! Praise Him for His goodness in suffering. Praise Him for His purposes and plans. Praise God for His eternal victory and triumph over sin, over Satan and over suffering. Praise God!

If you wish to contact me, I can be reached at either

jamiefreeman00@gmail.com

or

Jamie Freeman
P.O Box 741
Hackett, AR 72937
U.S.A

Also available from Christian Focus

BIG GOD

How to approach SUFFERING, spread the GOSPEL,
make DECISIONS and PRAY in the light of a God
who really is in the DRIVING SEAT of the world

ORLANDO SAER

ISBN 978-1-78191-294-2

BIG GOD

How to approach SUFFERING, spread the GOSPEL, make DECISIONS and PRAY in the light of a God who really is in the DRIVING SEAT of the world

ORLANDO SAER

There are so many problems that never get solved that it is easy to avoid the problem of answering them – but walk through your doubts and your questions with Orlando Saer as he explains the problems of pain, suffering, evangelism, guidance, and prayer. Understand the big picture as you walk through the why? in your life.

If God has seemed absent, He might start appearing for you in surprising places if you take on board Saer's words here. Accurate, biblical, clear, short, serious and practical... thinking meets life.

Mark Dever

Senior Pastor of Capitol Hill Baptist Church and President of 9Marks.org, Washington, DC

Cosmic practicality ... he peels off the cultural shrink-wrap from this massive doctrine and thus gives wings to Christian living - and mission. Here is medicine for the soul!

R. Kent Hughes

Senior Pastor Emeritus, College Church, Wheaton, Illinois

Orlando Saer is the Senior Pastor of Christ Church Southampton where he is involved in training and discipling university students. He has previously served churches in Sydney, London and Surrey. He is the author of *Iron Sharpens Iron* and *Big God*. He is married to Libby and they have four children.

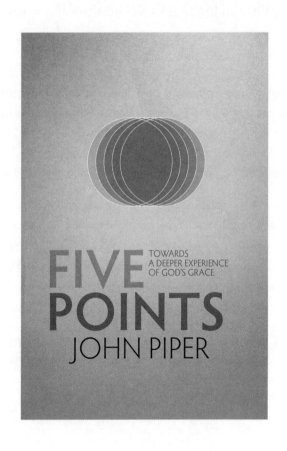

FIVE
TOWARDS
A DEEPER EXPERIENCE
OF GOD'S GRACE

POINTS
JOHN PIPER

ISBN 978-1-78191-252-2

FIVE POINTS

Towards a Deeper Experience of God's Grace

JOHN PIPER

Grace is the heart of God to do you good when you deserve it least. But do we really know how deeply we don't deserve it? Only God can reveal that to us. He does it through the Bible. And when He does, the wonders of His grace explode with brightness as never before. These Five Points are about how Christians come into being, and how we are kept forever. It reaches back into times past when we were freely chosen. It reaches forward into the future when we will be safe and happy forever. It reaches down into the mysteries of the work of Christ, purchasing the gift of faith for all God's children. And it reaches into the human soul, glimpsing the mysteries of the Spirit's work as He conquers all our rebellion and makes us willing captives of King Jesus. Piper believes that our experience of grace grows with our grasp of God's gracious work. He invites us to come with him on this quest.

> *I don't know of any other brief book on this subject that so manifestly takes us down into the Scriptures and then so wonderfully lifts us up to see the glory of God. Many people will be encouraged, and not a few will have their faith jolted in the best way possible.*

Kevin DeYoung
Senior Pastor, University Reformed Church. East Lansing, Michigan

John Piper served as pastor of Bethlehem Baptist Church, Minneapolis, Minnesota for 33 years. He is the founder and teacher of desiringGod.org, a chancellor of Bethlehem College & Seminary, and has written more than 50 books including *Desiring God* and *Don't Waste Your Life.*

the
Way
of the
Righteous
in the
Muck
of Life

Psalms 1-12

Dale Ralph Davis

ISBN 978-1-84550-581-3

The Way of the Righteous in the Muck of Life

Psalms 1–12

DALE RALPH DAVIS

In the opening pages of the Psalms, believers discover foundational truth for right living – and great delight – as children of God. Trusted theologian Dale Ralph Davis leads readers through a careful study of Psalms 1-12 with clear application for daily life.

The Psalmist begins with the most essential truth for mankind, Davis explains: 'Nothing is so crucial as your belonging to the congregation of the righteous.' And it is the Word of God that provides the direction for the believer's life. It is here, Davis points out, that 'the righteous man gets his signals for living.' The delight of the righteous is in the 'law' – the teachings – of the Lord. Indeed, for those who belong to Him, meditating on God's Word is 'the pursuit of pleasure'! The Psalms are a treasure trove for such a pursuit.

As the first 12 Psalms continue, we see basic principles unfold with great clarity. Much like our troubles today, the Psalmist endured wickedness all around, a world hostile to the true God-and on a very personal level – deceit and persecution from his enemies. Readers are pointed toward the glorious rule of the Messiah, to whom the whole world belongs. In light of this realization, we are prepared to face all kinds of troubles that cause despair. The righteous rely on God, and the Psalms teach us how. This book is ideal for use by small groups, as a teaching guide or for reference.

Dale Ralph Davis is Minister in Residence, First Presbyterian Church, Columbia, South Carolina. Prior to that he was pastor of Woodland Presbyterian Church, Hattiesburg, Mississippi and Professor of Old Testament at Reformed Theological Seminary, Jackson, Mississippi.

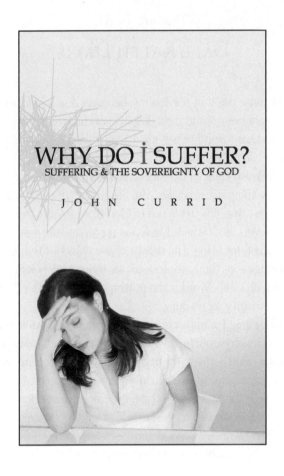

WHY DO I SUFFER?
SUFFERING & THE SOVEREIGNTY OF GOD

JOHN CURRID

ISBN 978-1-78191-506-6

WHY DO I SUFFER?

Suffering and the Sovereignty of God

JOHN CURRID

Why does God allow suffering?

It's a question that, in one form or another rears its ugly head time and again. Whether it comes from someone who has just lost a loved one, been diagnosed with an incurable illness or even just surveyed the plight of the poor in the third world. A few days after the terrorist attacks of 9/11 the question that was being asked around the world was – Where was God in this?

The question is one that has dogged Christians down the ages. A number of answers have been offered – and indeed all world views attempt their own response. John Currid brings Biblical teaching to bear. God does work in suffering, He is not a worried observer unwilling or unable to intervene, rather He has a purpose at work and is in control.

As Abraham said, "Shall not the Judge of all the Earth do right?"

Grasping that truth will help us as we face the future and ensure that when we are next faced with that most tricky of questions we will know where to begin.

John Currid is Carl McMurray Professor of Old Testament at Reformed Theological Seminary, Charlotte, North Carolina.

Christian Focus Publications

Our mission statement –

STAYING FAITHFUL
In dependence upon God we seek to impact the world through literature faithful to His infallible Word, the Bible. Our aim is to ensure that the Lord Jesus Christ is presented as the only hope to obtain forgiveness of sin, live a useful life and look forward to heaven with Him.

Our Books are published in four imprints:

CHRISTIAN
FOCUS

popular works including biographies, commentaries, basic doctrine and Christian living.

CHRISTIAN
HERITAGE

books representing some of the best material from the rich heritage of the church.

MENTOR

books written at a level suitable for Bible College and seminary students, pastors, and other serious readers. The imprint includes commentaries, doctrinal studies, examination of current issues and church history.

CF4•K

children's books for quality Bible teaching and for all age groups: Sunday school curriculum, puzzle and activity books; personal and family devotional titles, biographies and inspirational stories – Because you are never too young to know Jesus!

Christian Focus Publications Ltd,
Geanies House, Fearn, Ross-shire,
IV20 1TW, Scotland, United Kingdom
www.christianfocus.com